# LIVING WITH BIPOLAR

## My story isn't over yet;

## By G.L Warwick

MS G L WARWICK

I dedicate this book to my late grandmother
March 1931 to April 2018
I miss you every day and love
you more than anything
Forever in my thoughts
xxxxxxxxxxxx

# CONTENTS PAGE

1. The Early Days
2. Becoming a real adult
3. Motherhood
4. The House Fire & Divorce
5. The Diagnosis
6. How did I hide it for so long?
7. What is Bi-Polar?
8. What is EUPD?
9. Life after separation
10. The Cats
11. The happy ever after – 2018
12. The end of the happy ever after – 2019
13. Managing my mood
14. The Children
15. My diaries
16. Work
17. Obsessions
18. Relationships
19. Marriage
20. Sleep and Medication
21. Suicide
22. The Stigma
23. Nature vs Nurture
24. About Me
25. EUPD, Bipolar or My Personality?
26. Today, the year 2020, the future
27. Changes & Challenges
28. Relapse 2021

# INTRODUCTION

Depression isn't uncommon.

According to www.mentalhealth.org.uk almost one in five (19.7%) people suffer with depression in the UK.

***I am one of those statistics.***

Depression is a low mood that affects you for a long time and affects your everyday life. It's a persistent feeling of sadness and loss of interest in the things you enjoy. Depression is a constant feeling of being numb. You wake up in the morning just to go back to bed again. In its mildest form, depression can mean just being in low spirits. It doesn't stop you leading your normal life, but it makes everything harder to do and seem much less worthwhile.

At its most severe, depression can be life-threatening because it can make you feel suicidal.

Those who do not suffer from depression think depression is just sadness, but it is so much more than that. It also doesn't just affect mood but affects sleep patterns, physical wellbeing, cognitive abilities and gives a feeling of being anxious with a loss of hope.

**If you know someone who is depressed, please never resolve to ask them why. Depression isn't a straightforward response to a bad situation, depression just is, there is usually no real cause.**

I always knew something wasn't right. I was quite a shy child. I was often withdrawn and chose to have just a few close friends. I was happiest when I was closed away with my sewing machine. I would spend hours upon hours sewing! I also loved putting my roller blades on and just skating round the block again and again and again. I actually didn't mind my own company and hiding away on my own was something I quite enjoyed. This continued through my childhood and into my adolescence. I was very insecure and struggled in large group situations.

On the other hand, I also had a huge desire to please people and still do. I would swing from quiet and insecure to loud and energetic with an eagerness to impress and get everything right. My confidence was heavily affected if I was let down or if I experienced any form of failure. It was a vicious circle.

Confrontation was also a killer. I would cry for hours if I found myself in a hostile situation. I would never get into an argument I wasn't sure I was going to win. I'm still the same to this very day. I won't debate with you if I don't have lots to back up my reasoning. I also don't take criticism well due to my unhealthy desire to please.

I remember an evening after school sitting curled up at the end of the bed crying because my mum had criticised my grades and was comparing them to my younger brothers. I never felt like I was good enough. Sure, he was brighter academically, and his grades were indeed better than mine, but I was the creative one. My strengths were different fom his. This was the exact type of criticism that would make my mood spiral downwards.

I remember the occasion vividly and how I felt. As a result, I never compare my two. They are individuals with their own strengths, weaknesses and passions and these should be rewarded in the same way. Too much emphasis is put on academia and as a result sporting and creative achievements aren't treated the same. That day has stayed with me ever since. This must have been when I was about 13/14 as we were both at senior school.

Despite suffering as a teenager I had just turned 20 when I first went to the doctors about my mood. This was in Autumn 2001. I was very low. I would go to work, come home and then simply take myself to bed where I then slept until my alarm went off for work the next day. I wasn't eating, I had no desire to live and refused to socialise.

My life was work, sleep, repeat...

At the beginning of December after an argument with my then boyfriend I took twelve paracetamols with the intention of ending my life. I had instant regret and took myself next door to my neighbour who then contacted my mum and before I knew it, I was at A&E having blood tests. The next day, it was confirmed that my toxicity levels were within the normal range as the dose was actually relatively low, but I was taken back to the doctors for a review as there was concern about the suicidal feelings and any future attempts using higher doses or worse. The dose was low, but the intention was there. Next time it could have been worse.

During my visit to the doctors I was put on an anti-depressant called Seroxat along with a sleeping tablet called Promethazine and so, my battle with clinical depression began.........

I took myself off the anti-depressants after just a few months as I didn't like the way they made me feel. They made me gain weight, they made me sweat at night and I felt even more numb than I did before I was on them. I was also in a better place and felt like I didn't need them anymore. I then ended up back on them again the following year, again taking myself off them after a couple of months. I then completed this cycle of going on them only take myself off them a few months later again the next year. I then decided I was never going back on them again. By this point it was spring 2003.

Life continued with the usual milestones of jobs, university, boyfriends, travel, marriage and children with a few, not so usual milestones such as housefires and divorce.

At the start of 2016, when I was 34, I had a major breakdown. Everything started to feel like too much effort and my mood declined rapidly. I took myself back to the doctors and then in September 2016 I was signed off work for two weeks. This soon ended up six months and during this time my life was changed forever.

After spending all of my savings one week and then considering taking my own life the next, I was sent to Anchor House, the local Adult Mental Health Team, for further assessment.

Fast forward to the November of 2016 and after seeing 3 different psychiatrists and trying several medications I was given a diagnosis of Bipolar Type 2 with traits of Emotionally Unstable Personality Disorder.

The moment the psychiatrist said that I have EUPD my whole life suddenly made sense. The bipolar diagnosis was also welcome and a big relief. The diagnoses were actually quite liberating and eye opening. Whilst some people are mortified at their diagnosis I was over the moon. It had taken 20 years but I finally had the answers to why I felt the way I did.

Even the thought that medication will hopefully sort it all out was quite exciting. I was quite naive though because recovery needs so much more than medication.

These days taking medication is just a pain and I have to make sure I am strict with taking them. I have them in dosette boxes like the elderly do to ensure I don't miss a dose.

Taking medication is time consuming and exhausting. The side effects are awful. ***But they have saved my life.*** Without them I wouldn't be here to tell my story. That I can be sure of.

> *"Life isn't about waiting for the storm to pass, it's about learning how to dance in the rain"*

# CHAPTER ONE - THE EARLY DAYS

### *"How one handles success or failure is determined by their early childhood"*

In order to look at the present it is important to get an insight into my past. My past has heavily shaped who I am today and so I take you all back to the very beginning.

*A word of warning - whilst the rest of the book is neatly divided into chapters to make for an easy read I do sometimes jump backwards and forwards. One of my proof readers said she actually enjoyed this because it was a true represenation of my personality. I am yet to decide if this was a compliment or a back handed insult but either way I hope you enjoy 'Living with Bipolar; my story isnt over yet'.*

I am the eldest child with one brother and two sisters. I was born in October 1981 and my brother in September 1983. My brother and I share both parents whereas one of my sisters is from my mother's second marriage and my other sister is from my father's second marriage.

I grew up living on the (sometimes sunny) south

coast with my mother, stepfather, my brother and the elder of my two sisters, who was almost seven years my junior. My other sister was born when I was ten years old.

I remember them both being born and when I first met them both. I can even remember where they both were in the hospitals (their beds) and being very excited to meet them. My mum had got me a craft set to give me when I got to the hospital and we made paper chains in her hospital bed whilst my sister slept. I was only six and a half, but I remember it very well.

I was very happy both times to have a new baby sister. Well, that was until I realised I would have to share my bedroom with LW! She ended up a tom boy and so our room was decorated both pink & blue to suit us both! She was also quite messy as a child and snored very loudly!

Life from the outside looking in was pretty normal. My stepfather worked as a labourer at the local military base and my mother had a few part-time jobs which fitted around us children. I attended the local primary school and then at eleven I went to the local secondary school.

I did gymnastics, swimming and brownies outside of school and I enjoyed playing with my next-door neighbours. We made dens, camped in the garden, spent our summers dressing up and riding our bikes around the block. A pretty typical childhood in that sense. I did chores and helped my mum delivering her Avon orders and watching my sister when I got a little older.

On the whole, I enjoyed my primary years, but my senior school experience was pretty neutral. I did fairly well in classes and enjoyed learning but I found friendships hard.

I also participated in the choir, gym and dance shows and got involved in the school productions. I couldn't sing a note but what I lacked in talent I made up for in enthusiasm. I was quite good at dancing though and in year 11 I recieved the PE trophy for my participation and commitment to dance and gymnastics in the yearly shows!

I had lots of friends, but I never felt like I had a 'best friend'. I jumped from one friend to another. The group of friends I had are still really close to this day and I am still the outsider. I do, however, prefer it this way. I never was a fan of large groups and I have a couple of friends I still see from secondary school and that's it and I wouldn't want it any other way. Quality over quantity.

I also used to feel if I wasn't there then no one would miss me. Girls were bitchy. Boys were weird.

> *"I didn't like teenage girls even when I was a teenage girl."*
> *Cristina Yang, Grey's Anatomy*

My home life was also difficult. I shared a room with my sister which meant that, as she was so much younger than me, I didn't have much space to myself, particularly in the evening as she would go to bed much earlier than I did and so I actually spent most of my time at my Grans house. We would play Scrabble and watch our favourite movie 'The Sound of Music'. I would often 'run away' but after a while my mother stopped looking as she knew where I had gone. I worked out that if I ran fast and took the short cut through the houses I could get to my Grans before my mother even knew I was missing! I did occasionally mix it up a little and would go to my aunties house instead if my Gran wasn't at home.

My mother tried her best, but I did often feel frightened of her. I remember vividly her pulling my hair in a hurtful manner one day. I was sat in front of my wardrobe surrounded by its contents and she was shouting at me for something and she grabbed my ponytail. I don't remember what the issue was, but she was most likely taking her anger out on me from an argument she had had with my stepdad. This must have been in my teens as until I was twelve, I had short bobbed hair and it wasn't until then that I was allowed to grow it. I now believe my mother's aggression was down to her own undiagnosed and therefore unmedicated mental health issues along with dealing with my stepfathers demands in the home. I struggle to be close with my mother now I am an adult and it wouldn't surprise me if this is the root cause of it. I had no issues cuddling my Gran, it was one of my most favourite things to do!

This behaviour from my mother was quite mediocre in comparison to how my stepfather treated me though. He was a vile little man.

I have very clear memories of his physical and emotional abuse. I often say, if this was today then it wouldn't have been ignored and social services would have been involved but, being the early 90's this wasn't picked up on at school and as a result it was left to continue happening. I see many, many Child Protection letters at my job at the doctors and I just know we would have been on Child Protection for both emotional and physical abuse.

The one thing I should mention though is we were never neglected. We were always fed, clothed and given everything we needed and our basic needs were always met. Unfortunately, we would just be reminded of this fact quite often and we were forced to feel grateful we were being kept alive! A pretty basic requirement for an adult in care of a child!

He would scream, shout, be rude and abusive. I never did anything good enough. He was quite frankly evil and nasty, and he scared me.

I remember one day he had lifted me up by my

throat and was threatening me. I have no memory as to what I had done to anger him, but I do remember my brother screaming at him to put me down. AW's screams were clearly enough as he soon let go and dropped me to the floor. On another occasion he dragged me down the stairs and threw me across the room.

He was always clever enough to do this when my mother was out. He had a horrible temper and frightened me. As a result, I felt very vulnerable and was forever treading on eggshells. We would count the minutes until he came home from work, not knowing whether he would be in a good mood or a nasty one.

It made my life at home quite unhappy and I always felt like the unloved child. **My brother** being the only boy and highly intelligent was **my mother's favourite** and my sister being my stepdads only child was his favourite. With the way he treated me and how much my mum didn't know, it was hard to like myself and not feel in some way the left-out child.

**Objectively this may not have been the case but subjectively it certainly felt that way. I often joke, even now, that my brother is my mother's favourite child!**

On the flip side though, my stepdad did appear to have a caring side. He would stay up until I had got home of an evening to check I had made it home safely and he would regularly play taxi for me. Unfortunately, the bad outweighed the good. He was spiteful and controlling and I never really settled when he was around. He made my childhood and teenage years quite unhappy. Ironically though when my mum left him several years later, I was angry. I am not really sure why, but I just remember feeling like that. Shows how messed up I was. I do remember feeling angry that I had to the leave the house that had been my home my whole life and he got to stay there.

I now drive past him most Thursdays when I pick HC up from his sports club. He works nearby and he passes me on his bicycle. He knows it's me, he always looks into the car like he has recognised it. He scares me, even now. The glare, the look and the evil expression on his face.

This was another reason I spent a substantial amount of time with my Gran. **She was my saviour and she was the most amazing person I have ever met.**

I know everyone says that about their grandparents, but she took on so much more than a normal grandparent. She comforted me. She saved me.

In 2018, at the age of eighty-six, we lost her to advanced dementia, and I miss her every day.

We lost my grandad when I was twelve to lung cancer, and so my Gran became a widow at quite a young age, and I know therefore that she appreciated the company too, well except when I was beating her at Scrabble, which was actually quite often! I also loved a game of Boggle and Countdown, but she was better at both of those though.

Another productive thing that got me out of the house was babysitting. I was the eldest by quite a bit in the street and so I became the local babysitter and I prided myself in earning my own money from around the age of 14. I had regular families I sat for once a week and others I only sat for on special occasions. I enjoyed this very much and often think of the children, now adults, and how they are getting on. I even had an appointment book, and this satisfied the extreme organiser in me. I also vaguely remember writing up family profiles in a folder and I kept track of my earnings on an old school spreadsheet more commonly known as a pen, paper and a calculator. This was a skill I would later use when I became self-employed later in life, just on a larger scale than my babysitting records and with modern technology as opposed to the pen and paper method!

As I mentioned previously, I didn't grow up with my father living at home. He left when I was three and I would see him on a monthly basis but, this dwindled as I got older. I didn't have a very close relationship with either him or my sister. My stepmother, who I didn't like, made seeing my father very difficult. My mother also made it quite difficult for us to see him too so, I think he just more or less gave up. I wasn't overly affected as a very young child, but I do know I felt troubled and left out when he would take my sister on holiday to Florida and on cruises when I hadn't even been on a simple holiday abroad. Thankfully, this has now changed. Our relationship is still not that of a normal father/daughter, but it is now stable, and I no longer feel like the outsider that I felt growing up. The day I found out my dad and my stepmother had split up (in the latter part of 2011) I was elated! I liked her even less than my stepdad! She had taken my dad away from me and he had been replaced by my stepdad and we all know how I felt about him.

I now enjoy taunting my dad on his earlier life choices and congratulate him on his upgrade (his third wife CW).

CW brought with her four sons, so I now have four stepbrothers. I rarely see them though as they all work away and are hardly ever home. I think the last time I saw them was at Dad & CW's wedding when with a stroke of luck all seven of us children were able to attend.

I now also have a step brother and a step sister from my mothers third marriage.

I left school at sixteen with sub-standard grades, but I had at least achieved enough to gain a place in the sixth form studying a GNVQ in Health and Social Care.

My college days were strained though, just as they were when I was at senior school. I had a boyfriend (DS) who I met on our college residential to Wales just before we started Sixth Form. Despite having a serious relationship, I still chose to keep myself to myself at college and would hide away in the classroom at break times. I would see him outside of college though and I loved him to bits, and we had a really lovely 'first love' type relationship. I would sometimes socialise but on the whole, I preferred my own company. I also felt stupid. I was the only one in my friendship group doing a GNVQ and they were all doing A-Levels. I had a fear of embarrassment and failure. It was easier to just hide away and concentrate on my studies. I took very few friends with me from my time at school and even less when I finished college.

Due to my choice to be alone, I soon got ahead with my coursework and at the end of year one I was already working on year two work. The teachers encouraged me to attempt an A-Level in just one year. I chose Communication Studies and despite studying for this, I still managed to complete my GNVQ with five months to spare. I left college in June 2000 with a merit in my GNVQ and a D in my A-Level.

During my time at college I had several jobs. Sometimes a few at once.

I worked at the local preschool couple of mornings a week. The manager was actually one of the families I babysat for. I fitted this around my classes at college and gave me both work experience and money for driving lessons. I really enjoyed this role.

At the weekends, I worked at a local tearoom one day and at a hotel as a chambermaid the other. This was then the same hotel I then got married in many years later. I had admired the brides from afar during my time there and I made it my dream that if I was to ever get married that I would be one of those brides.

I always had to fill my time with either work, seeing DS, sewing or working on my studies. Any reason I could find to avoid socialising and from being at home and I would look for it. I also worked during the holidays at the local theme park in the catering department. I thoroughly enjoyed this role and after securing more hours I gave up the roles at the tearooms and the hotel. I ended up working there for five seasons and I loved every minute. My brother, sister, DS and half of my school year ended up working there too at some point. I take the children there on occasion now and it has changed so much since I worked there. I prefer it the way it was fifteen years ago, but my children love it either way. Every child loves a theme park and maybe they will both follow in my footsteps and end up working there too when they are older. It was a really lovely place to work. Some of the staff I worked with still work there now.

After college, I was a little lost. I had originally applied to university to study Childhood Studies and was accepted at both Chichester and Canterbury Kent universities. I then applied through clearing for a place on the same course at Sheffield University to be with DS. I decided in the end to decline all of these offers as I didn't feel ready. I really wanted to become a primary school teacher, but I couldn't without a C in my GCSE Science which, despite retaking in my first year of college I didn't achieve so I decided to go down the nursery nursing route.

I managed to secure a place at the local nursery doing an NVQ apprenticeship in Early Years Education. It still frustrates me to this very day that I needed that C grade because had I been born the year before then I wouldn't have needed it and I am still not sure why I needed a decent grade in science to teach floating and sinking to 5-year olds!

By this time DS had moved up north for university as planned and for the first year I would visit him every other weekend and so.... my life became nursery during the week, studying in the evenings and travelling up north to visit DS at the weekend.

After a year, the travel wore me down and we chose

to end things. I still think about him to this very day. Afterall, we were together 3 years and he was my first love, my first everything. Thanks to social media I am able to see he is happy and getting on well in this thing called 'life".

I managed to complete the two-year course in just six months and I soon became a qualified nursery nurse. After just a year though, I decided this wasn't for me after all. I still yearned for that career in primary education and so, I decided I needed a change whilst I worked out my next plan.

I applied for a job at a computer company as a receptionist. It was fairly local and the perfect fill in job whilst I got my head straight and thought about what I wanted to do career wise. I was lucky to get this role and soon settled into a routine working there.

The company was largely male dominated, and before long I realised that I much preferred working with men as opposed to women. Working with men seemed to suit my personality better as there was less bitchiness and no stabbing behind peoples backs. Men were much easier to work with and as a result I suffered less self-esteem issues and was overall much happier.

I also loved flirting with them. It was all in jest though and just part of working with a large bunch of men. We all knew it was fun and just made the day go quicker. I also socialised more than I ever did. Playing Twister at our christmas party in a very short skirt with a team full of men after too many WKD's probably wasn't one of my finest moments though!

Ironically my self-esteem raised working there. I enjoyed taking the mickey out of my boss and mocked him on a daily basis. I was born to work with men!

After an 18-month break from my studies and the career planning and after quite a bit of soul searching, I decided I needed to try re-taking my GCSE science again (one last time) and go to university after all.

I chose a fairly close university so I could live at home. I was three years older than the majority of the students and my lack of desire to make friends, live in halls and live the university dream meant it made sense to stay at home. I attended university simply to attend lectures and use the library.

I started in September 2003 and chose to study Early Years Education with Social Care at Winchester University. I was lucky enough to continue working at TCS on the helpdesk and as an unofficial PA to the operations director. I had a great working relationship with both him and one of the project managers and we still keep in touch to this day. Albeit not enough. Big Ears B and Half a Job H!

My work and university schedule was full on. I

would work mornings if I had an afternoon lecture and an afternoon if I had a morning lecture. It worked very well and I worked more or less full-time hours. Weekdays were work and lectures, evenings and weekends were for studying. I was able to earn and study at the same time.

Despite the heavy workload – both in my employment and at university - I managed to stay on top of my university work obtaining good grades all whilst progressing at work too. I became obsessed with my university work though. It was all I would do.

Obsession is another symptom. More on obsessions later on.

After I split with my 'first love' (despite it being an amicable decision to end things) I became very low and convinced myself that he would be my first and only love and I would never find love again.

When DS and I went our separate ways, I became quite promiscuous jumping from one boy to another. These two years were also my first two years at TCS. Little did I know at the time, but this was a symptom of my now diagnosed bi-polar. I won't reveal quite how many I shared my time with so as to not admit my sins to the rest of the world, but I definitely enjoyed these two years. I visited friends at their universities and had 'fun' there, I had found myself attracting the attention of a group of friends (not all at once I would like to add) and at work I was friendly with a guy from accounts. I had also got back in touch with a guy I had met whilst working at the theme park a few years previous and we met up to get rid of years of tension that had built up. It wasn't worth the wait though!

Any attention and I was happy to oblige.

This, however, wasn't the true me. This behaviour was just signs of my illness. Hypersexuality is a real thing. It's an unspoken symptom of bi-polar. It isn't something that people like to admit to themselves.

After each encounter I would drop low and struggle to carry on. I would hate myself and I would feel ashamed.

Until the next time....

This rapid cycling is yet another symptom. It was all there from an early age. The mood swings, the promiscuous behaviour, the unhealthy attachments to boys who at the time made me feel like a million dollars only to abruptly take that away from me leaving me to spiral downwards again. I never did learn my lesson! I still haven't!

I was also very sexual from a young age and remember exercising my sexual curiosity as a teenager even though I didn't really know what I was doing until much later on in my late teens. I just knew it felt nice and I needed to do it. These were again, all unnoticed signs.

Whilst my depression wasn't documented in my medical records until 2001, when I was twenty, it most definitley started before this. If I was on 'edge' and anxious I would attack my bedroom. I would pull out my wardrobe to reorganise it, I would move my room around and I would make all my friends cushions. Everything I owned would be categorised into number, colour or alphabetical order. When I was a teenager, I used to buy nail varnishes so they all matched, I collected small plastic bags (rather embarrassingly I still have the collection stored in the same box I did all those years ago) and my hectic cleaning was so renowned I would be asked to tidy my friend's rooms for them when I was in the mood. I was usually happy to oblige. I also had an obsession with pins, badges and lanyards and I still do! Anything to occupy my mind.

A few days after this I would crash, and I wouldn't be interested in life anymore. My mum said I was always hyperactive when I was tired and would not stop talking. When I think about this though, I realise I wasn't actually tired – I was hypermanic and the crash after was the depression. This was misinterpreted as tiredness and normal teenage moodiness, although, I am sure hormones did have their part to play as well.

My history with being put on anti-depressants and taking myself off them when I felt good again, only for the cycle to repeat itself months later was also a symptom.

Between birth and 2003 I had quite a few significant life events. My mum and dad divorced (which back then was quite a rare thing), they both remarried and there was the birth of my new sisters. Again, having half siblings was rare back then. I was the only one in my friendship group to come from a broken family (until our early teens at least anyway). This was the common term used back then for children whose parents had broken up. These days the terms 'modern family' or 'blended family' are used and these are far nicer. I then, had the school issues and the college issues. The fitting in issues. The career and university dilemmas. A girly holiday which turned out to be a bitch fest. A holiday with my first love. The end of my first love and the promiscuity that followed. I also had the broken heart that would mend itself only to be broken again. I took lots of risks and laughed lots. Of course, there was also the physical and emotional abuse I endured at home during my childhood and then into my teens and early adolescence.

All in all, both my childhood and adolescence were quite memorable but for lots of different reasons. Some of it was great and some of it was very bad.

Despite all of this I came out the other side, albeit **broken**, infact very broken, **but alive.**

# CHAPTER TWO – BECOMING A REAL ADULT

*"We're adults. When did that happen?*
*How do we make it stop?"*
*Meredith Grey, Grey's Anatomy*

In Sept 2003, just before I started university, I met MC at the local pub. I had known of his family for years as we went to the same schools and his father was heavily involved in the local football team that my brother played for. He also has an unusual surname and everyone in the area had at least heard of them. We, on the other hand, had never officially met. I did however have crushes on half of his friendship group as a teenager, as did most of my friends. He was a bit like me, part of the cool gang but not even remotely the 'coolest' one!

I started university a couple of weeks after meeting him and began to enjoy the beginning of my new relationship and studying again. Life felt settled and I was happy.

Despite everything falling into place, the time period I was at university wasn't uneventful. I was doing well in all my modules and I was thoroughly enjoying studying again and work was really good too.

Rather frustratingly though in my first year I failed my GCSE science **again** and so I finally abandoned the dream of becoming a primary school teacher. Looking back now though I am quite grateful as I'm not sure the teacher life is for me but I guess I will never know.

Then, in Feb 2005, my mother and stepfather separated. By this time, I was in my second year of university and my mum and I moved out leaving my sister with her dad (my stepdad). In hindsight though, we should have taken her with us as life became unbearable for her in the end. He moved his new partner (his now wife) in, with her son too and she started to make life awful for her. Her dad chose to take his girlfriend's side in every disagreement they had and so, in 2007, LW moved out and she hasn't spoken to him since. My brother had already sensibly moved out by this time and was living abroad away from all the drama. In 2011 I had to speak to him for what I hope was the last time. This was on behalf of my mother and this was due to a disagreement over their divorce papers. It was quite nice being an adult and being able to stand up to him a little. Even if he was still a bastard and scared the crap out of me.

Unfortunately, during my third year, my father in law passed away suddenly just after Christmas after suffering cardiac arrest. I remember the day vividly. I supported MC and his family the best I could but of course whilst all of this was going on, I was also working more or less full time and maintaining good grades.

In early 2006, shortly after his passing, we purchased our first house. A little two-bedroom house with a tiny garden. It wasn't much but it was ours. We spent months making it our home.

Despite all of that I graduated in June 2006 with a 2:1 with some fancy letters after my name. I went back fulltime at TCS and started to train as a project manager. I also began to study for the Prince 2 Project Management qualification. I attended meetings in London with my boss where I felt important in my suit and heels! I was really enjoying life. I had my career, my own home and my whole future with MC ahead of me. The next few months were uneventful and I was enjoying the boring side of life!

In October 2006, just after my graduation ceremony, MC sat me down and told me about an opportunity that had arisen for him to take a contract in Malaysia to assist with opening up an office for the company he worked for. There was a new office full of new procurement staff and he was sent to essentially teach them the job. This was a huge decision to make but after a 'trial' week there we decided to go for it. One of his colleagues said,

**'regret going, do not regret not going'** and I have used this phrase often since.

So, in April 2007 we packed up our belongings into the loft or sent them to Malaysia in a metal box and rented our home out and off we went. It was weird going away not knowing when I would next be home, but it was exciting, if not a little bit nerve wracking too. I remember crying at the departure gate as we were waiting to board.

We rented a three-bedroom apartment right in the middle of the expat community and a few minutes' walk from the main shopping centre. It was a beautiful place to live with a collection of swimming pools and plenty of space for visitors. MC's commute to work was much nicer than his UK one too.

The next year was amazing but it wasn't without its flaws. Homesickness was regular but this was outweighed by the amazing experience of living abroad. Due to visa restrictions I was unable to work out there, but I was allowed to work as a UK employee. So, I worked a few hours a week remotely for TCS doing some tasks I was able to do from abroad despite the time difference. This kept me in touch with work and that actually proved useful on our return. It also gave me a reason to get up in the morning, the sunbathing soon got boring and it also gave me a little bit of my own money. I had been earning my own money for years and I wouldn't have liked being 'kept'. It was only pocket money, but it gave me the chance to contribute a little bit.

I also made some wonderful friends and we had lots of visitors grateful for the free accommodation and the wonderful tour guides!

I was also lucky enough to visit many countries during this time. We spent a few days in Japan visiting my brother who was there on a year contract as an English teacher. Japan was a slightly weird country but amazing and I feel privileged to have travelled there. I loved the authentic Japanese elements to the country such as when we visited Kyoto where all the temples and women in their traditional dresses were, but Tokyo was big, crazy and busy. We also visited Osaka which is where my brother was actually living, and I loved that city. We then took the bullet train back to Tokyo and that was quite an experience.

We visited Hong Kong for my 24th birthday where I spent the day at Disney! I loved Disney (who doesn't!) and also the popular tourist spot, Stanley Market, but I didn't enjoy the rest of Hong Kong. It was like London, crowded and expensive but just much hotter!

We did a day trip to Macau which was fun. I went to Thailand twice managing to visit 4 different areas which included the very busy Bangkok, Koh Samui, Phuket and the beautiful Phi Phi.

I wasn't overly keen on Thailand, but it was nice to tick it off the bucket list. I felt it was too commercialised and dirty. It just wasn't my cup of tea.

My favourite place was Singapore. This was simply awesome. The zoo, the city and Sentosa Island. It was all perfect.

We also visited Kuala Lumpur on the mainland several times and Langkawai, a small island not far from the island of Penang where were living. I loved Langkawi.

It was a short plane or boat ride from Penang, but it was worlds apart. The beaches were beautiful.

Our year living away gave me the travel bug and I have managed a fair amount of travel in the last ten years. I've been to New York, St Lucia, Dubai, Italy, Shanghai to visit my brother twice and Australia and I have also re-visited Penang and Singapore. With two of my siblings living abroad I foresee lots more travel in our future. I love travelling and I love even more that my children have already exerienced a decent amount of travel in their short lives and we have all made a list of future places we want to visit.

### "Travel makes you modest. You see what a tiny place you occupy in the world"

The year was fairly stress free for me and I could manage my own time according to my mood. Not that I realised that's what I was doing at the time. I would work in the morning, visit the supermarket in the afternoon and use the time to prepare for our upcoming wedding by handmaking the invitations and organising the favours.

I made the bridesmaids handbags and jewellery too. Naturally my sewing machine had travelled with me to Malaysia. One benefit of living in Asia was the supplies were cheap and I had plenty of time on my hands. One of my favourite things to do was to put the aircon on full blast in the apartment and snuggle up on the sofa under the duvet with an afternoon of movies. This made me feel at home when I missed it.

After just one year there we were sent home as the job was done. I was both happy and sad at the same time. I was homesick but equally I had just got used to the life there and was starting to enjoy the adventure. We had also made lots more travel plans which would now have to be abandoned and not to mention the friends we had made. Most of these are now all back on their own home soil and scattered across the world but we all still keep in touch, even if it is largely on Facebook.

We returned home on a wet rainy day at the beginning of April with two weeks of staying at MCs mums house ahead of us whilst we waited for our tenants' contract to end and for them to vacate our home.

It was difficult adjusting to life back home. There was of course, the weather changes, I was working again so had less freedom and everything was now costing so much more. Penang felt like a distant adventure and the U.K felt uninspiring. I was, however, fortunate enough to return on a fulltime basis at TCS. By this point I had been working there in the many different scenarios for 6 years. Considering it was only supposed to be a stop gap job back in 2002 and it was now 2008, it was clear I couldn't stay away.

By this time, it was May 2008 and we were due to get married in the September so, along with adjusting to working life again the wedding plans were in full swing. September soon came around and our wedding day was perfect. The weather was stunning, and the day was amazing and of course, I looked beautiful!!

Just a few weeks after an amazing honeymoon to New York and St Lucia, we discovered I was expecting our first child. She was due in July 2009.

The pregnancy was fairly uneventful (with the exception of a hideous rash called Pruritic urticarial papules and plaques of pregnancy, or PUPPP for short! Google it, it's horrible) and she was born happily and healthy on time, even if she did cause me a little bit of hassle making her way into the world. She was a stubborn little monkey and needed a little of extra assistance in the form of forceps with an excessive amount of blood loss (1100ml) and a nice postnatal infection in my stitches.

She was worth it though. She is now a happy little lady who loves learning and always has a smile on her face.

Unfortunately, during my pregnancy, TCS went into administration and we all lost our jobs. I was devastated. That place was like my home and my colleagues were like my family but, I had the rest of my pregnancy and being a mummy to look forward to. Watching my tummy grow was magical.

I stayed at home with our daughter for the first 9 months. I found these quite lonely and yet rewarding too but it was soon time for me to return to work. I found a part-time job at a small family run company where I attended to the admin jobs. We also purchased our second home, a three bed round the corner and this was perfect timing as just 9 months into my time there, I found out I was pregnant with our second child. A boy due in August 2011. I went on maternity leave and never returned to that role.

He was also born on time and healthy and thankfully arrived in a slightly less dramatic way than his sister. He was, however, the perfect example of how two babies are never the same and often the first child gives a false sense of security because, HC landed in our lives with a big bang and definitely woke us up. Literally! He never slept!

He is still a little whirlwind but is full of character and loves his sports and general boyish activities. He never sits still and makes us laugh every day. He makes me cry a little bit too!

There I was 30 years old with everything I have ever wanted. Married with two children, the pigeon pair with a lovely home and the fortunate option of being a stay at home mum.

# CHAPTER THREE - MOTHERHOOD

*"Being a mother is learning about strengths you didn't know you had and dealing with fears you didn't know existed"*

I soon settled into my role as a mother of two. I loved both my children dearly but I'm not ashamed to admit I struggled. It wasn't the magical experience I thought it would be.

If we went out, I would get overwhelmed. I enjoyed spending time with them at home but when I attempted something outside, I would go into full panic mode. I even struggled taking them to the park. I felt like everyone was watching and judging me.

I never settled when we were out. I hated it. I also struggled to 'play' with them. I was able to do things like crafts with them as this was structured but when it came to playing dress up, playing with cars and games.

I struggled. I didn't feel connected in the way I should have. I still struggle to play with them now.

Thankfully the make-believe phase has passed but you will never find me bouncing at a trampoline park! I also hate taking them swimming but it's hard to explain why.

I also **hated** toddler groups and other groups where other mothers gathered together. I found them clicky and uncomfortable.

I did manage to attend a post-natal group after I had OC where I made friends with a few other mothers with babies the same age who also lived in the village. Two of them are still very close friends to this day and I have been very grateful for their friendships. We celebrated our ten years of both mummy hood and friendship with a drunken camping weekend last summer and it was very special, even if it did rain most of the weekend. The children are like siblings and whilst they now have their own friendship groups due to having developed their own interests and personalities, they are still all such good friends and still look out for each other. Just like us mummies do. Its times like that that I actually enjoy being a mother.

This was the only group I went to though and this was because it was run by health visitors and it was a structured six-week information course. It wasn't mothers just sitting round talking and comparing who has the better 'behaved' baby and who has lost the most weight because they are pro breast feeders and their baby will never have a drop of formula. It was a kind of 'lecture' type format where we sat in a circle with our babies on our laps and the health visitor would impart her knowledge on to us. We learnt about weaning, vaccinations and we had ADVICE on breast feeding and various other subjects. No judgements, no clicks.

Despite finding the confidence to attend the course though, I still lacked the confidence for toddler groups and other mother baby classes. They simply didn't suit my personality.

The confidence to attend such groups was also affected by the way I perceived myself as a parent. I felt like I didn't live up to the way a mother should be. I considered myself useless. I always felt like I was judged by others and it was safer to stay at home where I could be the type of mother I was beginning to be, despite whether that was the way the books told me to do it or not. I still do feel like this. I worry what people think of the way I parent now the children are older. HC has some issues with socially acceptable behaviour, and I worry it reflects badly on me, so I choose to stay home more than I choose to go out. Although this is probably judged too. OC doesn't go to any clubs and neither can swim properly and I am aware this is probably judged too.

> **"Successful mothers are not the ones who have never struggled. They are the ones**

**that never give up, despite the struggles"**

When they were little and I wouldn't have to go out to do school runs I could spend days in my pyjamas, and I would simply put the lazy day down to a bad night with HC (who refused to sleep) and general motherhood stresses. Looking back, I can now see this was all post-natal depression. When I saw the psychiatrist many years later, I took my mum with me the first time and she admitted that she thinks I had PND. I was slightly upset that no one told me and made me get help back then. Maybe I would have done things differently.

I was desperate to be a normal parent. I desperately wanted to love being a mother. I loved my children and seeing them grow but I shouldn't have found motherhood this difficult.

My second lot of maternity leave ended, and I wanted to go back to work but it wasn't worth it with two lots of childcare. I was also lucky in that financially we didn't need me to work but in order to bring in a small income and, to find more purpose in my life, I registered as a childminder. I missed the independence of having my own money and having a life beyond being a mother, wife and housekeeper.

On the whole I enjoyed this, however, I realised I missed adult interaction more than I thought I did and so I applied for a bank staff role at a local children's charity (www.honeypot.org) that my sister worked for. My other sister ended up working there too but much later on after I had left.

I enjoyed the role and the flexibility the bank staff contract offered me. I could work as often or as little as I wanted. I used to go to work for a rest! That was my day off from being a mother. A day just for me, even though I was working.

I would accompany the mini bus driver on Fridays to collect vulnerable children and young carers and help deliver them to a purpose built home in the forest where for 48 hours they got to play, learn to ride bikes and for some children it was a chance to have a cooked meal and even a good night's sleep. It was a very rewarding role and the work they did was amazing.

I loved seeing the children's faces light up at the sight of the cows and horses as we entered the forest. Many of these children came from severe poverty and lived-in high-rise flats in very run-down parts of London.

I had worked there for around 2 years when I chose to leave. I thoroughly enjoyed the role, but I decided to leave in order to concentrate on my small sewing business. A promotion for MC also meant that the few pounds I earnt each month weren't worth me working a weekend and missing out on family time.

With both kids now in nursery & school I was now

able to have some time to myself during the week now and could meet up with friends' (kid free) to gain that adult contact time I needed. I also used this time to also concentrate on my sewing. This doubled up as both an income and me time because for me sewing is relaxing and good therapy.

I had originally started selling my sewing products as a pocket money job, but it ended up very successful with a strong following on Facebook. Sewing had a been a large part of my childhood and I loved finally making money from it. I was actually asked when making my career choice at an earlier age why I never chose a textile-based college course and pursued a career in that area, but the answer was quite simple. I wanted sewing to stay a hobby and I didn't want to end up doing alterations all day. I loved nothing more than being surrounded by beautiful fabrics and pieces of paper full of ideas. I like to create and start from scratch. I wanted to still love sewing and not grow to eventually hate it and have it feel like a chore.

After a few months I purchased a fancy new machine and had a cabin built in the garden to use as my sewing office and I threw myself into that. The cabin is now affectionately known as 'The Craft Cabin'.

I loved being self-employed and spending my days surrounded by pretty fabrics. I created my own brand 'S&S" and my unique selling point was called

'Build a Bag' where customers got to design their own bag. They could choose the fabric, the closure, the pockets, the size and even the straps. It proved very popular and I did very well. I then expanded my brand even further to include my own patterns and in 2018 I added craft parties (The Craft Cabin on Tour) and lessons to my service.

I now have a website and my daughter got on board a couple of years ago and we added Scrabble frames to what we make. It was her idea and she does quite well from them. My little crafter and entrepreneur.

*If you haven't noticed the pattern by now, I was forever changing my path and throwing myself into every new idea or venture. This was also a symptom of my unrecognised bi-polar diagnosis.*

Life ticked along.

However, it was during this time that I became obsessed with running and weight loss. As **with many bi-polar sufferers' obsession is common**. I managed to lose 4st and achieve pretty good personal bests with progression from group 4 to group 2 at a running club in an incredibly short space of time. I raced every race and attended every session. I joined the committee where I was soon membership secretary, race secretary and website administrator.

I counted every calorie and weighed myself every

morning. If I hadn't lost weight I ate less and exercised more. At my smallest I weighed 8st with a BMI of 19 and I was wearing a size 6-8 clothing. I was actually proud of my extremely skinny frame. I technically had a borderline eating disorder. I was never skinny enough and I was determined to get even skinnier. I remember telling the doctor how much weight I had lost and then subsequently gained once I was on my medication and she said that she was pleased I was putting weight on because I had got too small and it wasn't healthy. I didn't agree but the medication had other ideas. The medication has now unfortunately achieved a fabulous victory and I've given up trying to win that race!

This was, again, another obsession. One that took over my life. At least the sewing obsession made me money though. The running obsession cost me instead!

Whoever says running is free is wrong. I needed lots of trainers for various terrains and weathers, many, many running outfits, a head torch, a fancy running watch, running bras, race fees, running club fees…… the list is endless.

*Despite all of this, life still ticked along.*

**Then 2014 happened. The year 2014 was the start of my diagnosis. The real start of this story.**

**My past has shaped my future but ultimately it was 2014 when the official journey began.**

**Everything started to slot into place, my diagnosis was revealed, and my recovery began.**

# CHAPTER FOUR - THE HOUSE FIRE AND THE DIVORCE

The first episode in which I can now recall was in July 2014. There was a last-minute space on a 24-hour relay event with the running club and I was determined to get this place. It was over a whole weekend and four hours away **and** it was the following weekend.

Normal G would have analysed the situation and recognised that I simply hadn't done enough training to do this event but the (now recognised) bipolar part of me became obsessed with the idea and **I created a path of destruction in order to go.**

MC was away that weekend on a friend's stag do so I begged my mum to have the kids and did everything I could to ensure I could go.

The weekend was actually amazing. I managed three laps of six miles, and I felt elated to have achieved this with very little training. It was this weekend that also made me fall in love with camping. When I came home my mood suddenly dropped. The high of the weekend had gone and I was left with 'life' again.

The summer ticked along, and I trained for my first half marathon which was in the September. I trained hard and whilst the race wasn't as successful as I had hoped I still managed to keep the finish time under 2 hours. The disappointment of the finish time made me more determined than ever to train and get quicker and stronger.

I carried on training, being a mother and a wife and working on my sewing business.

**Unfortunately, in November 2014 our house suffered a fire**. I had been out just 45 minutes when I returned to find my house on fire. I originally thought maybe I had left my hair straighteners on and that is why I could smell burning. I walked upstairs and realised the lights weren't working. That's when I came face to face with the fire in my bedroom. I ran downstairs somehow losing my glasses in the process and I called 999 screaming down the phone "my house is on fire, help my house is on fire".

Some of my neighbours came out and waited with me for the fire engine. It was the longest 12 minutes of my life waiting for that engine to arrive, watching helplessly, as my house was burning.

It was truly a life changing moment, and nothing would prepare for me for what we saw after the fire was put out. The whole of upstairs was black. My bedroom was pretty much burnt, and the rest of upstairs was severely smoke damaged. The cause of the fire was a lamp that had overheated. This had been purchased in China.

*Pro tip – don't buy cheap Chinese electronics. They are liable to catch fire!*

The rest of the evening was a bit of a blur. The shock had 'told me' to drop the kids at my mums (where we then stayed for a few days) and then head out to running club as per my original plan. I missed the run, but I went to the pub wearing my smoke covered clothes. I now know this was incredibly selfish, but the kids were asleep, and the **shock told me to go.** I do feel guilty now, looking back. It was a very stupid and selfish decision. Shock does funny things and I had no rational thoughts at all.

**"Psychological shock is when you experience a surge of strong emotions and a corresponding physical reaction, in response to a (typically unexpected) stressful event"**

The damage was extensive, and we were required to move out of the property whilst repairs were put in place. The whole contents of our house were either restored and then kept at a storage facility or disposed of. We moved into a small flat just a few hundred metres from our house whilst the work was completed.

Naturally I went into major breakdown. Anyone in this situation would have. I cried for months. I would be happy then sad. I drank lots, cried lots and laughed lots. My running obsession got even worse as I trained for more and more races.

The year 2015 however, was the year of personal bests. I managed 47 minutes for a 10k. I shaved off almost 25 minutes (from 2 years before) for 10 miles and ran that in 1 hour 20 minutes. I took 10 minutes off my half marathon time (from just 6 months before) and I also managed a 6 minute 40 second mile.

My proudest moment during my running obsession was running over the finish line of a 24-hour relay race after completing my 7th lap of 5 miles and helping my team (of 5) finish 10th out of 79 places. The feeling was exhilarating, and I was invincible. I wore my medal with pride.

The time in the flat was overall tough but after 6 months we were able to move back into our home.

Furniture was re-built, and life was re-stored. We celebrated our first night back with a curry from our favourite Indian takeaway and a bottle of wine. It was so nice to be home again.

However, we had a secret.

**Prior to the fire we had separated** but as it was amicable (we had simply grown apart) we had decided to wait until after Christmas to make it official. We wanted to give the kids one last family christmas and I needed time to find a part time job. The fire prolonged this action though and we chose to keep it a secret until we were back home and had settled the kids. They had had too much upheaval for one year already.

We had been on a holiday to Dubai in September 2013 to celebrate our 10-year anniversary and I realised on that trip that something was missing. Life afterwards just wasn't the same. I battled with the loneliness for another year and finally in September 2014 I made a hasty decision to end my marriage. No discussion. Our marriage was over.

In hindsight this rushed decision was out of character for me and a rational version of me would have discussed it and possibly found a resolution but my 'super power' attitude at the time gave me the confidence to believe I would be fine on my own with the children and I didn't think of the practicalities of being a single mother and that most importantly that **maybe we could attempt to find a resolution** to our issues.

Looking back now, I do know we would have separated anyway but maybe in a different and less brutal way! MC always used to say that I would be very good at analysing things such as whether we could afford a new car or what is the best TV and I would spend months researching but once I had made my decision I had to go and buy it there and then. The same with the separation, a whole year of deliberating and then bang, a final decision just like that with no care or thought and with mainly selfish reasons. It was what I wanted and that was it! **Another symptom perhaps??**

We settled back into our home and normal routine whilst I sought employment in order to aid the separation process. My sewing was doing well but this income was sporadic, and I needed a regular income again. Going back to work after 4 years of temporary roles and self-employment was strange and extremely nerve wracking but I was excited.

I updated my C.V and began the search. I found myself a role, quite quickly, in a local doctor's surgery near where I grew up. I started working there as a registration clerk in September 2015 and I became a single mother in the October. The role was simple, but I enjoyed it. After just a few weeks I was given a different role (Clinical Coder) which I had for 5 years before leaving in December 2020.

I was fortunate that whilst I am now a single mother, I have good support from my ex-husband. He has the kids regularly and we co-parent very well. Naturally it's not perfect but we make it work for the children's sake and we have been commended for the way we co-parent ensuring the children's needs come first. We spend Christmas eve and Christmas morning together every year.

After all, there are only so many magical christmases and we didn't want to have to divide them up. We also attend school and sporting events together. He has even visited whilst we have been camping a couple of times and the kids love that. We also do their birthdays together. None of this 'two of everything' lark. The split was amicable so there is no reason why this couldn't happen. Given I grew up with a mother and father who refused to speak to each other, I was determined to make sure that despite our split that our children didn't have to go through that too.

Life again.... ticked along. *Working, motherhood, co-parenting, dating and battling to make each day count.*

# CHAPTER FIVE - THE DIAGNOSIS

*"Diagnosis is not the end, but the beginning of practice"*

The year 2016. The year of the diagnosis. The year my life suddenly made sense.

It was April 2016 when I found myself suffering from depression again. It had laid dormant for several years and it had come back with a vengeance.

I spent my days at work with a fake smile on my face but by the evening I wished I was dead. Work colleagues thought I was shy and quite blunt (I found this out much later on at an appraisal) but in reality, I was simply just getting through each day with minimal contact so as to hide my sadness. I went to work, did my job and came home again. A little bit like I did in 2001 when I was first diagnosed with depressionn.

I was simply existing.

It went work, kids, sleep....repeat and I didnt even have the desire to do that let alone anything else.

When I was able to tell my friends and colleagues

months later about my diagnosis, they were all shocked – they all had no idea how I felt as soon as I opened the front door after a day at work. My friends felt awful that they hadn't noticed and that I had suffered alone but that's the thing with depression. It's easy to hide when need be.

> **"You keep yourself to yourself because it's difficult to find people who understand and it's much easier to fake a smile than to explain what you really feel"**

It all started 'officially' again after an argument with my then boyfriend. I use this term loosely because as you will read, he wasn't the best boyfriend. This was the first guy I saw after my separation and who I had met at running club and the relationship just kind of happened. I certainly wouldn't swipe right on him given the chance now! He is 100% not my type!

The argument was over the fact I was sat in my car outside his brother's house (who he was house sitting for at the time) and it was cold and I was hungry and he was once again late without a care in the world for me and my time. I later found out that he had 'popped' to the pub on the way home from running club despite the fact he knew I had gone straight there and would be expecting him to be right behind me given we left at the same time.

I was understandably upset and angry but being the selfish bastard he was, he managed to make it all my fault and he then chose to ignore me all evening. This wound me up even more (he knew which buttons to press) and I walked out.

My intentions weren't to drive home, they were to drive to the nearest bridge and drive off it. I sat in the car sobbing for quite some time, hoping he would come out to see me, but he clearly didn't care. I took the keys and started the ignition. I spotted a lamppost in the distance and fully intended to rev my engine and drive straight into it as fast as I possibly could. Thankfully sense came over me, I pulled the keys from the ignition, threw them on the floor and calmed myself. I then finally drove home and went to bed. My heart was pounding, and tears streamed down my face until I eventually fell asleep.

I would like to point out, this guy was 20 years my senior **(running off with a much an older man – that was most definitely a symptom!)** with 3 grown daughters and should have known how to treat me better. I would often ask how he would feel if his daughters were treated in this way, but he was always good at changing the subject.

I felt I deserved to be treated like this though and simply put up with it. He managed to convince me everything was my fault and I was simply a 'psycho'. A psycho because I wanted to be treated better and with respect.

Whilst the incident wasn't actually my fault (he

was selfish with a lack of respect for me) I knew something wasn't right. I reacted in a very suicidal way to the situation. To get upset was one thing but to become actively suicidal was another.

So, the next day I took myself to the doctors and was given Sertraline, the most commonly prescribed anti-depressant.

This worked for a while, but I soon became tolerant to each dose and before I knew it, I had been titrated up to the maximum dose and I had gained 2.5st almost overnight. Whilst my mood had lifted slightly I had lost interest in running and so with this sudden drop in exercise and the new medication, my weight escalated quickly. The doctor gave me another SSRI to try – this time Fluoxetine.

I am undecided as to whether this worked. It certainly didn't help with the weight gain issue that's for sure. My mood had lifted which was good but within a few weeks I had my first (now) recognised hypomanic episode. This was quite possibly triggered by the antidepressants, which is another common sign of bipolar.

According to www.healthonline.com antidepressants alone aren't always the most effective treatment for bipolar because Antidepressants increase the amount of neurotransmitters in the brain. Serotonin, norepinephrine, and dopamine are 'feel good' chemicals that lift a person's mood and reduce depressed feelings but the use of antidepressants for bipolar is controversial because they can trigger a manic episode. They should always be used with a mood stabiliser and/or an anticonvulsant medication (more on medication later).

This hypomanic episode was in the August (2016). I spent all of my savings in one week. This was on random stuff that I didn't really need, dresses, bags, a cross trainer (which naturally I ended up using just a few times before selling on) and 2 cats, well 10-week-old kittens to be precise. I swam, walked, went to a spin class with a friend who said she struggled to keep up with my speech and I cleaned the loft at 1am. I had a very high sex drive. I made a zillion plans and I filled my diary with tons of things. I found myself in every supermarket in the area, The Range, Ikea, on eBay and Amazon. I treated the kids to Lego. Purchased loads of fabric and a new bed for HC.

During a hypermanic episode I buy pretty things, I make changes to the house, I spoil the kids, scrub the house and make all sorts. I also have this issue in that I am unable to purchase something in one colour or style. The same as I used to do with the nail varnishes when I was younger! I had to get every colour going and they had to be the same brand, so the bottles all matched.

Those who knew me well questioned my sanity when I announced I was buying two kittens. I was not a pet person. I was too house proud. I was the last person you would expect to get a pet. I wouldn't change them for the world now (more on cats later) but it was a strange thing for me to agree to and it certainly turned a few heads.

Shortly after this week I became very low and wanted to die. All I wanted to do was sleep, eat crap and wish I was dead. I didn't want to speak to anyone, see anyone or do anything. I literally did the school run and that was it. I had no food in the house, and we survived on food from the bakery and the small co-op in the village as I couldn't bring myself to go to the big supermarket or even do an online shop. I found myself on several occasions googling how many paracetamols it would take to end my life and when I didn't have the children, I would drink lots.

I managed to talk to one of my oldest friends, who, I should say, at the time worked for the NHS providing CBT to inpatients and is now studying for her PHD in Clinical Psychology, about my sudden mood change from very high to very low. I told her about my midnight cleaning, my increased sex drive, my hyperactivity and then my sudden suicidal feelings. She suggested I may have more than unipolar depression. She told me midnight cleaning the loft was not normal (who knew!). My moods were too erratic and were at either end of the extreme. Someone with unipolar depression doesn't go through the "highs" of bipolar depression and it was clear I was suffering from these highs too.

I took myself back to the GP and explained what my friend had said and mentioned her profession to give her opinion some credibility. The GP signed me off, this time for a month and then referred me to Anchor House, the local Mental Health Team, for further assessment.

To my surprise, my appointment came very quickly and just a couple of weeks later I was sat in front of a psychiatrist spilling my heart out with my family history and the reasons why I had been referred. I remember my legs constantly shaking as I sat in the waiting room. I felt sick and wanted to be at home. I remember being that nervous that I changed my outfit loads of times and ended up settling on something that made me look like I was going for a job interview.

After what felt like a year and a million questions, I was given a mood diary to complete. This is a simple yet effective way of diagnosing a mood disorder. I was unmedicated during this time (just a low dose of SSRI's as they had more than halved the dose I was on) and so the mood diary was very true to life.

I was asked to score my mood each day. This would be from 0-10, 0 being severely depressed and 10 being manic with no grasp on life. This is known as the 'mood scale'. www.bipolaruk.org/faqs/mood-scale

Ideally a score in the green box is preferred (numbers 4-6) and this is where a person with no mood disorder would score themselves.

A patient with Bipolar Type 1 will score themselves as high as number 10 but not quite as low as zero.

A patient with Bipolar Type 2 will score themselves as high as number 8 but will go as low as zero. I have been in these sections of the chart many, many times.

| | | |
|---|---|---|
| MANIA | 10 | Total loss of judgement, exorbitant spending, religious delusions and hallucinations. |
| | 9 | Lost touch with reality, incoherent, no sleep, paranoid and vindictive, reckless behaviour. |
| HYPOMANIA | 8 | Inflated self-esteem, rapid thoughts and speech, counterproductive simultaneous tasks. |
| | 7 | Very productive, everything to excess (phone calls, writing, smoking, tea), charming and talkative. |
| BALANCED MOOD | 6 | Self-esteem good, optimistic, sociable and articulate, good decisions and get work done. |
| | 5 | Mood in balance, no symptoms of depression or mania. Life is going well and the outlook is good. |
| | 4 | Slight withdrawal from social situations, concentration less than usual, slight agitation. |
| MILD TO MODERATE DEPRESSION | 3 | Feelings of panic and anxiety, concentration difficult and memory poor, some comfort in routine. |
| | 2 | Slow thinking, no appetite, need to be alone, sleep excessive or difficult, everything a struggle. |
| SEVERE DEPRESSION | 1 | Feelings of hopelessness and guilt, thoughts of suicide, little movement, impossible to do anything. |
| | 0 | Endless suicidal thoughts, no way out, no movement, everything is bleak and it will always be like this. |

*An extract from the psychiatrist's letter after my*

***first appointment**- "G presented today as a well kempt lady wearing a skirt and a shirt. She maintained poor eye contact during our consultation and was anxious and tearful at times. She was restless and was moving her arms and legs whilst speaking, although maintained good rapport. Her speech was normal in rate, rhythm and tone. She described her mood subjectively as 5 out of 10; objectively I felt it was lower than this. She has a full insight into her high and low moods. I feel that this is a chronic mood instability and is most likely bipolar. G will keep a mood diary to confirm the diagnosis"*

I started my mood diary that day. My lows were very low. No lower than before really but giving the mood a score highlighted just how low I was. I would wish I would get poorly, like really poorly. I wanted to get poorly so I would die so the pain would end or at least so I could be hospitalised enough to be able to avoid real life for an extended period of time. Physical illness is also seen as less taboo than mental illness and is objective. To die from a physical illness felt a better way to go. My death would be treated differently if I had died through a phsyical illness as opposed to taking my own life.

Physical illness is diagnosed through scans, tests and examinations. Mental illness is diagnosed based on mood diaries and the trial of many medications. If a medication helps with the depression and in the case of bipolar, the hypermania, then a diagnosis can be made. To be off work with a physical illness seemed less embarrassing and more believable than being off with a mental health condition.

I still feel like this to this very day. To be off work with a physical illness usually means a bunch of flowers and a get-well card, to be off with a mental health condition though usually means you are ignored whilst you are off and your ability to work efficiently questioned upon your return. Well this was my experience anyway.

There is now of course the explaining of my mood disorder to prospective "suitors" on dates and this has been very nerve wracking and embarrassing. No one wants to be with the crazy girl so I down play it to begin with and hope that if/when I have an episode that they know the real me well enough to know it's just my illness and it will pass soon and I will be back to my normal self soon.

**After several appointments, medication changes and trials and an extensive mood diary I was formally diagnosed with bipolar disorder type 2 with traits of emotional unstable personality disorder.**

This was in November 2016.

*Truly a life changing diagnosis.*

Suddenly everything made sense. All of my 35

years explained in one meeting.

# CHAPTER SIX – HOW DID I HIDE IT FOR SO LONG?

***"I hide my depression behind a big smile. I like to be the reason people are happy"***

So, my depression laid dormant and unnoticed for several years and I believe there are a few reasons as to why. This was largely down to the distribution of my time – between work and children and having my Gran as support.

Before I had the children, I was able to manage my moods easily as I only had myself and work to incorporate into my day. If I was sad, I could hide away. I could go to sleep and get a full night's unbroken rest. At weekends I could lay in or have days on the sofa.

As soon as I became a mother though, my sole responsibility was my children. They needed constant entertaining and I couldn't rest. If they were awake so was I. My routine was also all over the place which is something that ended up an important factor in how my mood is managed (more on that later).

I **had** managed to work fulltime prior to having the kids but due to the role I had at TCS, if I was fidgety, I could change the role I was doing to suit my mood. I could hide away doing quotes and work for my boss if I needed to be quiet or I could pull out the filing cabinets and help tidy areas such as the workshop, to occupy my mind if I was 'hypermanic'. I had 6 different roles during my time there. Some ran parallel to each other. I started as a receptionist, spent a huge chunk of time on the helpdesk dealing with customers IT queries and directing to them to our engineers whose diaries I also managed. I was an unofficial PA to the operations director, and I was training as a project manager. I also spent some time with the development team and thoroughly enjoyed learning about basic coding.

Another role I had and one I very much enjoyed was, working with the engineers on many of our customers sites moving and installing computer hardware. I enjoyed wearing my steal toe capped shoes and hard hat on the sites and my heels and suits in the day in my role as trainee PM.

I was never satisfied with **just one role** though and thoroughly enjoyed the variation. **This was definitely a symptom.**

Then, once I became I mother I didn't work regularly. I was able to choose my own hours depending on my mood and I could hide away with my babies when the outside world didn't look appealing.

**This all helped with the <u>cover up</u> and I believe this is how I was able to hide it for so long.**

Working properly again in 2015 definitely heightened my mood swings and I couldn't hide them away anymore and this ultimately led to my breakdown in 2016. My cover was suddenly blown, and my emotions were out there for everyone to see.

**This of course was also the first time I was both a mother and working regular hours again. Until now I had only done one or the other.**

The last and main reason I believe I managed to hide it for so long was the relationship I had with my Gran. As you know I was very close to her growing up but even as an adult with young children and my own home I still needed my Gran for emotional support. She was my outlet. I was able to pour my heart out to her and this meant I hid most of my emotions on her shoulder.

She suffered a major stroke in early 2014 and suddenly she was gone. Not physically but mentally she wasn't here anymore. I had no one to lean on, no one to share my worries with. She was the only constant in my life and suddenly Gran, as I knew her, was gone and my emotions had nowhere to hide anymore.

Writing this, at the age of 39, I have tears in my eyes. I get tearful whenever I think of her. She was my number one.

I was lucky to have her share lots of big events in my life such as my wedding and the birth of both my children, whereas my siblings and cousins weren't so lucky.

However, she has also missed out on so much too. I missed her terribly when my house caught fire and my marriage broke down. She was still alive at this point but her advanced dementia meant she wouldn't have been able to understand if I told her so I simply didn't and as a result I couldn't visit her. She couldn't comfort me, and I found it hard to see the once extremely happy and high-spirited woman reduced to a life without memories sitting in her chair at the care home. She didn't know who I was and that killed me.

Family members would criticise me for my lack of visits, but I chose to remember her the way she was, the way she made me feel and the way she comforted me.

I now know that this sounds incredibly selfish but the four years she survived after her stroke were the worst four years for me too and I couldn't find the strength and courage to see her. She was never far from my mind though and still never is. She was and always will be my most favourite person ever.

I often dream of her. I dream of her orange tablecloth and her piles of magazines. I dream of the sleepovers I had and the tea & toast she insisted I had in bed before getting up. I sometimes smell her. I loved her smell. She would always wear a cuddly cardigan and snuggling into her with her soft floral smell was like heaven. In my Gran's arms was my most favourite place to be.

When she died, I left this letter in her resting place......

*To my dearest Gran, the day you had your stroke my heart broke and the day you gave up your fight my world crumbled. I have so much I want to say yet my mind is speechless. I still can't believe you are gone. You were the kindest most caring amazing lady I have ever had the privilege of having in my life. I was so lucky to have you as my Gran. You made me who I am today. I am who I am because of you. I will never forget everything you did for me growing up.*

*As I write this, I am watching The Sound of Music and it makes me smile. The Sound of Music was our thing and I am pleased to say that OC loves it too now as well. I might take her to Austria one day. I am so glad I got to share that experience with you – nearly 14 years ago now. That trip is definitely one of my favourite memories of our time together. Even if you were a pain at times!!*

*I have so many other wonderful memories*

*too...... The Cotswolds, the Meerkats, Jersey, your red tartan blanket, the orange tablecloth, arctic roll, fish in sauce, your smell, your cuddles. How you would bring me tea & toast in bed whenever I stayed over. How you taught me to play the organ. Milk Jelly. Our holby city Tuesdays. Countdown. Your sweet, biscuit & cake stash, gold bars and classic bars. The bowl of fat in your fridge and the way you always had frozen milk and a tub of real butter. But most of all your kindness and how you were always there for me. You rescued me when I 'ran' away from home and then when you let me stay with you when I needed somewhere to stay for a few months. For that I will be forever grateful.*

*My two most memorable memories though are the hours and hours we would spend playing Scrabble and then seeing how proud I made you at my graduation.*

*I am sorry I haven't been there as much over the last few years, but your stroke broke me, and I simply couldn't deal with seeing you deteriorate as quickly as you were, but you were never far from my mind.*

*Since your stroke, so much has happened in my life. So much I wanted to tell you and share with you and it broke me knowing you didn't even know who I was.*

*You had your stroke in early 2014 and since then*

*I have experienced a house fire, MC and I separated, I started a new job at the local doctors. I then had a manic breakdown with a diagnosis of bipolar. This led to a 3-year turbulent relationship with an older man that I made the decision to end just a few months ago.*

*I truly believe you held on until I was feeling more stable and no longer suffering so I could cope with the loss of you. Whilst I have been unable to talk to you about my troubles and share things with you, I was able to feel comfort in knowing you were there. I've had some dark times Gran, but I have come out the other side and for the first time in a long time I am happy and feeling grateful to be here.*

*I will miss you every day and I still can't believe you have gone but Grandad and Trevor needed you. I expect Trevor has been causing Grandad some trouble and he needed your help.*

*Until we meet again Gran xx*

*Love you more than anything xx*

*Thank you for being a wonderful, caring and amazing Gran xx*

*Forever in my heart x*

I now have a special tattoo on my foot. It is a yellow flower (she liked daffodils) and the quote "Climb every mountain" next to it. Climb every mountain is from The Sound of Music and was her favourite song from the film. I also like the meaning of the lyrics. In the movie, the mother abbess is convincing a younger nun to follow her heart. It is a very powerful song in the film. I now have a forever memory of her, of our favourite film and our favourite song etched on my skin.

The irony is she would have hated the tattoo though!

> *"Climb every mountain, Ford every stream,*
> *Follow every rainbow, until you find your dream"*

# CHAPTER SEVEN – WHAT IS BIPOLAR?

So, what is bipolar? According the NHS website, Bipolar disorder is a mental health condition that affects your moods.

Moods swing from one extreme to another. It used to be known as manic depression. People with bipolar disorder have episodes of depression and hypermania. There is no test for bipolar and for guidance, doctors and psychiatrists use a book called 'The Diagnostic and Statistical Manual of Mental Disorders' or you have probably heard it referred to 'The DSM'. This presents the diagnostic criteria for bipolar and many other mental health disorders.

Approximately 1 in every 100 people will be diagnosed with bipolar at some point in their life. Bipolar disorder can occur at any age, although it often develops between the ages of 15 and 19 and rarely develops after 40. I was 35 when I was diagnosed and I was 19 when it all began.

There are 3 types of bipolar – **Type 1, Type 2 and Cyclothymia.**

**Type 1** involves periods of severe mood episodes from mania to depression. Mania is the same as hypomania but usually involves hallucination, psychosis and often requires hospitalisation (remember the mood scale)

**Type 2** is a milder form of mood elevation, involving milder episodes of hypomania that alternate with periods of severe depression.

**Cyclothymia** is a mild form that includes brief periods of hypomanic symptoms alternating with brief periods of depressive symptoms that are not as extensive or as long-lasting as seen in full hypomanic episodes or full depressive episodes.

**I have Bipolar Type 2 so my 'highs' don't get as severe as those with Type 1 but my lows are usually much worse.**

# What is a "MOOD DISORDER" anyway?

⭐ **BIPOLAR I:** ALTERNATING MANIC + DEPRESSIVE EPISODES

⭐ **BIPOLAR II:** ALTERNATING HYPOMANIC + DEPRESSIVE EPISODES
  ↳ "HYPOMANIA" = MILD MANIA

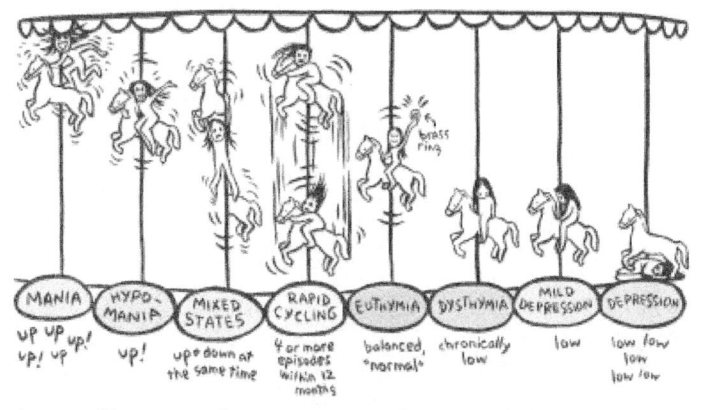

| MANIA | HYPO-MANIA | MIXED STATES | RAPID CYCLING | EUTHYMIA | DYSTHYMIA | MILD DEPRESSION | DEPRESSION |
|---|---|---|---|---|---|---|---|
| up up up! up! up | up! | up + down at the same time | 4 or more episodes within 12 months | balanced, "normal" | chronically low | low | low low low low |

According to the DSM, to be considered hypomania, the mood must last at least four consecutive days and be present most of the day, almost every day.

https://www.psycom.net/bipolar-definition-dsm-5/

During this period, three or more of the following symptoms must be present and represent a significant change from usual behaviour:

- Inflated self-esteem or grandiosity
- Decreased need for sleep

- Increased talkativeness
- Racing thoughts
- Distracted easily
- Increase in goal-directed activity or psychomotor agitation
- Engaging in activities that hold the potential for painful consequences, e.g., unrestrained buying sprees

The depressive side of bipolar disorder is characterised by a major depressive episode resulting in depressed mood or loss of interest or pleasure in life. The DSM-5 states that a person must experience five or more of the following symptoms in two weeks to be diagnosed with a major depressive episode:

- Depressed mood most of the day, nearly every day
- Loss of interest or pleasure in all, or almost all, activities
- Significant weight loss or decrease or increase in appetite
- Engaging in purposeless movements, such as pacing the room
- Fatigue or loss of energy
- Feelings of worthlessness or guilt
- Diminished ability to think or concentrate, or indecisiveness
- Recurrent thoughts of death, recurrent suicidal ideation without a specific plan, or a suicide attempt

**There isn't a straightforward answer as to what bipolar 'looks like' though. Just like cancer and other physical illnesses. Neither are easy to generalise. Bipolar displays itself differently in everyone. The same as cancer will spread differently for every patient.**

An episode however, for me, looks something a little like this....

It will start off with a couple of nights unable to sleep well, my mind will be whirling with all kinds of ideas. I get fidgety, restless and I feel my mood start to rise but not necessarily in a good way. I know I am about to trigger when the keyboards bother me at work, and I can't keep up with conversations. It's when I have to stick both headphones in. Before I know it, I am overtired, overwhelmed and overstimulated. Once I am at this stage, I am in full hypermanic mode. **I will be awake, determined and full of energy.**

Once the tiredness kicks in, my mood will drop literally overnight. I will be snappy, irritable and extremely low. I will hate myself. I will want to die. I will stay like this for around 2 weeks until suddenly the cloud lifts and I am feeling normal again.

When I am hypermanic I have to get everything in order. Sleeping is a waste of time. Eating is a waste of time. I make lists. Lots and lots of lists. I sort emails. I sort paperwork. Throw out clothes, toys, makeup.... you name it, I will sort it. **I often joke**

### 'don't sit still or I will clean you too'!!

I will clean and scrub. I make plans, promises and spend, spend and spend. My OCD tendencies become more apparent and my whole life will be categorised! I buy things on impulse. I find noises annoying and people frustrate me. I will have some great idea about a new career or something. This idea will be the idea that saves me. This one is the one that will be my final idea. It will make me money. It will make me happy.

I will take risks and when I am single, I will be promiscuous.

I also pretend I am super mum. Let's make a cake or do some sewing, its only 9pm! I remember taking the kids out to the cabin about 8pm one night and we covered the walls with colourful handprints. It took hours and looked very cool but was totally uncalled for at that time of night.

When I am hypermanic I hate food shopping, but I will go to enormous lengths to find the perfect purple, floral, shiny clock to match the new lampshades and new bedding I just had to buy. I will drive wherever I need to go to get that matching clock. The scrapes in the side of my car are as a result of needing to get matching boxes for my unit from ikea and the world would have come crashing down had I not got them.

By nature, I do like things to match but I wouldn't

go out of my way when I am low or normal in the same way I do when I am hypermanic.

I have made other errors when I have been hypermanic such as painting our front door bright red (we no longer live there but 10 years later the door is still red!) and then spilling paint on the carpet because I couldn't wait to paint the spare bedroom. Waiting for help was wasting time.

I have also ended up with my own bumps and bruises with no idea how I have got them. I also managed to tear the ligaments in my ankle because I was rushing down the stairs and slipped very awkwardly. I was on crutches for a couple of weeks and I still get pain in the ankle, even now.

I see specks of dust everywhere, I hoover behind units, empty the wardrobes, turn the whole house upside down and can often be found cleaning the shower whilst I am in it and naked!

I have simultaneous tasks and lists going at the same time and I become very forgetful. I race past people at the school as though I am trying to dodge a marketer outside on the high-street because I don't have the time to chat and if I do stop to talk my speech will be rapid and I will speak before I think and I will rarely remember anything discussed in that conversation.

The psychiatrist noticed a difference in the way I would write my lists and diaries depending on what mood I was in.

Hypermanic diary writing would be long rambling typed on my phone and printed off and my to-do lists were scruffy and all over the place.

My low mood diaries were scribbles and very short entries, yet my lists were neat and tidy but usually not very long or detailed.

I become very creative but not necessarily productive. I can't handle it when someone messes with my plans and organisation. I become obsessive and demanding, everything must be done exactly as and when I need it to be. Everything has to be perfect. I get crazy eyes and have been told in the past that I look a bit mad!

This hypermanic episode usually lasts around 3-5 days. I achieve lots in this short space of time!

***I then come crashing down and suddenly I am depressed with no will to live.***

When I am depressed, I will sleep 18 hours a day. My memory becomes foggy and I lack concentration. I hate myself and everyone around me. I hate work. I shake. I become quiet and withdrawn. I become snappy and want to hide away. I want to give up on life and I become very suicidal.

I go on a mission of self-destruction and seem to have this skill of messing things up even more. I will look at photos of my wedding and I'll find memories of my Gran. I will look at pictures of me as a size 8 and I'll look at my bank account and work out how much money I don't have. I'll think of everything that could have been and I see everything in front of me as a negative. I'll create situations to make it worse for myself. I will start arguments with people, I will treat myself to something and then regret the spending, I'll eat shit and then feel angry for doing it so I will then starve myself which of course make things 10 times worse. I end up in a bigger hole than when I started.

It's technically a form of self-harm, emotional as opposed to physical but self-harm all the same.

According the NHS, self-harm is when somebody intentionally damages or injures their body. It's usually a way of coping with or expressing overwhelming emotional distress. The intention is more often to punish themselves, express their distress, or relieve unbearable tension.

The clean tidy house that was so important last week no longer matters and the lists I created are thrown away. I stop washing my hair. I spend the next two weeks in my pyjamas with no bra and my hair is usually unbrushed. The bed sheets I changed daily last week will now end up staying on the bed for the next 2 weeks. I drink alcohol to numb the pain. Lots and lots of alcohol.

After a drink or four I will sit there with tablets

in my hand. I wouldn't necessarily want to die but equally I wouldn't want to be there. Tears will stream down my face. Why did I feel like this? Why couldn't I just be normal? I have 2 healthy children, a job, friends and family. Surely this is enough?

The only thing is, during moments like this, none of these positive thoughts would enter my head. Rational thinking is something I am just not capable of at that moment.

I will spend my days in bed watching boxsets, breathing heavily, crying, eating junk food and feeling irritable. This all lasts around 2 weeks and then once I am feeling better, I am left to clean up all of the mess I created during the episode. I am likely to have made mistakes at work, neglected the house and avoided friends. I have to repair all of this following an episode.

If I am lucky my mood will return to normal almost overnight and I will like my life, I will like my job, I will like my kids, I don't obsess about my weight, I dress normally, shop normally, clean normally and I shower normally. I start to care again, and my memory improves.

When I say normal, I mean I no longer clean at midnight or refuse to clean at all. I clean the perfect amount to keep the house tidy but not enough that it affects my life.

***Sometimes, however, just to mix things up a little I***

*have what is referred to as a mixed episode or mixed state.*

*I will wake up and not know what mood I am in.*

This is where I am depressed but with lots of energy. According to mind.org.uk a mixed episode is described as when you experience symptoms of depression and mania or hypomania at the same time or, quickly one after the other.

The mixed episodes are the worst. They are the most unpredictable and most dangerous ones because it is during a mixed episode that suicide is likely to occur. A patient who is depressed does not have the energy to commit suicide whereas a patient in a hypomanic state will be too happy to consider suicide.

**Both states together mean you are depressed but with the energy to commit that suicide.**

During a mixed episode I will clean like I am hypermanic but cry whilst I do it. My skin will feel like its crawling. I will get irritable and get in the car and drive for hours. I will angry clean. I have energy but angry sad energy. This is the most dangerous state for me to be in.

During a mixed episode, I will drink a bottle of wine without it touching the sides. I would wish there was more so next time, I would buy a box instead. Drinking however, doesn't make things better or disappear. Drinking makes me cry. Drinking makes me sob. Drinking during a mixed episode makes me actively suicidal.

A mixed episode for me can swing from anger, irritability, happy, tearful, suicidal, productive and impulsive. I can get all of these emotions and feelings in just one day. I will want to hit things, I will become paranoid. I will want to cry, laugh and scream. I will want to stab someone or myself. I will be snappy. I won't eat or I will eat too much. I make lists, pull cupboards out and do lots of online shopping. Mixed episodes are quite exhausting!

Many people think bipolar just affects your mood, but this isn't true. It can also affect your energy level, judgment, memory, concentration, appetite, sleep patterns, sex drive, and self-esteem. Additionally, bipolar disorder has been linked to anxiety, substance abuse, and health problems such as diabetes, heart disease, migraines, and high blood pressure.

**An amusing visual description of the two extreme sides of bipolar I found on google.......**

# LIVING WITH BIPOLAR

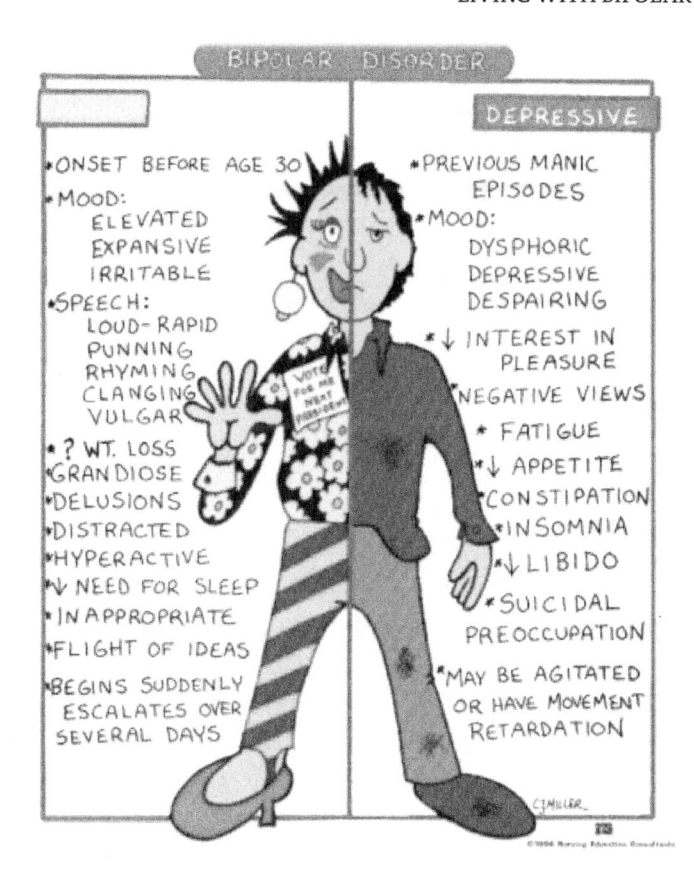

## BIPOLAR DISORDER

### [MANIC]
- ONSET BEFORE AGE 30
- MOOD:
  - ELEVATED
  - EXPANSIVE
  - IRRITABLE
- SPEECH:
  - LOUD-RAPID
  - PUNNING
  - RHYMING
  - CLANGING
  - VULGAR
- ? WT. LOSS
- GRANDIOSE
- DELUSIONS
- DISTRACTED
- HYPERACTIVE
- ↓ NEED FOR SLEEP
- INAPPROPRIATE
- FLIGHT OF IDEAS
- BEGINS SUDDENLY ESCALATES OVER SEVERAL DAYS

### DEPRESSIVE
- PREVIOUS MANIC EPISODES
- MOOD:
  - DYSPHORIC
  - DEPRESSIVE
  - DESPAIRING
- ↓ INTEREST IN PLEASURE
- NEGATIVE VIEWS
- FATIGUE
- ↓ APPETITE
- CONSTIPATION
- INSOMNIA
- ↓ LIBIDO
- SUICIDAL PREOCCUPATION
- MAY BE AGITATED OR HAVE MOVEMENT RETARDATION

# CHAPTER EIGHT – WHAT IS EUPD

So, because life wasn't happy enough throwing just Bipolar at me it chose to give me traits of Emotionally Unstable Personality Disorder (EUPD for short) too.

EUPD shares many characteristics with bipolar. For example, someone with EUPD may be impulsive, irritable and argumentative. The difference between the two though is that moods shifts with EUPD are typically abrupt, short lived and **almost always in response to an external trigger** such as a conflict with someone else. Bipolar mood shifts are slower to develop, last longer and not usually in response to anything in particular.

With EUPD, one will cycle rapidly and will move from despair to euphoria in a very short time. It is very difficult to manage feelings of abandonment, anxiety or anger, and it is common to harm yourself in various ways, either physically or mentally. It is common to "self-medicate" with alcohol or drugs, or to develop eating disorders or engage in self-harm. **Ring any bells?**

Your self-confidence may be okay sometimes, only to plunge into deep self-hatred the next minute and you may have difficulty trusting and feeling secure in close relationships, and you may frequently swing between admiration for the people closest to you at one minute and contempt for them at the next. This can make it difficult to maintain relationships in the long term.

Many people with borderline personality have had an extremely traumatic or chaotic childhood and some have been abused. **Remember my childhood?**

According to the criteria, in the DSM you should have at least five of the following symptoms to be diagnosed with EUPD,

- An intense fear of abandonment.
- A recurring feeling of emptiness.
- A confused or unstable self-image.
- Sharp fluctuation between different moods: Strong irritation, fear or depression that may last from a few hours to a few days at the most.
- Stormy relationships that swing between intense admiration and extreme contempt.
- Intense, heated anger that is disproportionate to whatever triggers it.
- Short-lasting, excessively suspicious ideas or temporary feelings of detachment from

reality.
- Impulsiveness that leads to abuse of drugs, sex, food or money, for example.
- You harm yourself, have suicidal thoughts, talk about or plan to take your life.

Management of EUPD is slightly different to Bipolar. Anti-depressants help with the depression but recovery and managing EUPD is identifying the problems in that persons life that could be triggering the disorder.

Psychotherapy is the primary treatment for borderline personality disorder. Cognitive behavioural therapy (CBT) is a type of psychotherapy used for treatment of BPD. This type of therapy relies on changing people's behaviours and beliefs by identifying problems from the disorder. CBT is known to reduce some anxiety and mood symptoms as well as reduce suicidal thoughts and self-harming behaviours.

# CHAPTER NINE - LIFE AFTER SEPARATION

The years 2014 to 2017 were my life changing years. The years that taught me a lot about who I was and what I truly wanted from life.

The main events of course were....

2014 – The Fire
2015 – New job & The Separation
2016 – The Diagnosis
2017 – The Recovery

I returned to work in early 2017 after 6 months off and a couple of months after my diagnosis (in Nov 2016). I was very nervous to begin with. Infact, in all honesty, I was a wreck. My anxiety was telling me everyone hated me. I would be the black sheep.

To aid the return, I came into the office a couple of times to see the team and to help with my first day nerves. I struggled to settle back in initially, but soon enough, I was back into a routine and it was like I had never been off, let alone for so long.

However, I was by no means 'fixed'. I was still seeing the psychiatrist every couple of weeks and my medications were still being changed in order to find the magic combination.

I also rapid cycled lots during the year 2017. Looking back at my diaries, confirms this. One day I was hypermanic, the next I would want to die.

Rapid cycling, according to the NHS, is where a person with bipolar disorder repeatedly swings from a high to a low phase quickly. There is no normal in between. This is similar to a mixed episode.

I have taken on a slightly different stance with this chapter. I have chosen to share diary entries from 2017 in order to give you a closer insight to what I actually thinking a lot of the time during an episode.

Just a few of the crazy entries from my diary during the year 2017....

> "ooh is it morning yet? I want my new duvet cover!"
>
> "my feet are moving, and my brain is alive. I need to google things, what can I google? Oh, I think I will write a book"
>
> "things are starting to arrive from my epic spend last week – why did I buy 10 metres of ribbon? What on earth did I have in my head to do with it"
>
> "ahh I ordered lots of travel wallets that all

match, well done G"

"irritable as fuck today. Cleaning lots. Kids arrrggghh. Want to cry. Want to move the house around. Even the cats are arrrggghhh"

"hoovered, swept, cleaned, hoovered more, washing, dishwasher, uniforms, shoes, boxes, paperwork and kids' rooms"

"drove to work but barely remember the journey. I do however remember wanting to crash my car"

"tearful on the way to work. Putting on the brave face but really want to go home and cry"

"the to do list I've made is ridiculous"

"its 00:30 and I am thinking I might get up and paint the small border fence out the front. I really wish B&Q was open so I could go and get the stones I need for the garden. I want it all now!!!!"

"worked out in the last 5 nights I have only had 20 hours sleep'

"removed my notepad from my desk and I instantly felt lost. I have come to realise that my notepad of lists is my way of coping"

"EVERYTHING a struggle today. Eating, moving, walking...EVERYTHING" "heart is pounding, noises are aggravating me"

"I want to die. I really just want to die"

"my life is so fucked up"

"today has been a drive all day kind of day"

"I find certain people can tip me over"

"if I rest too much that triggers me, if I don't rest enough that triggers me"

"only the 4th day of the summer holidays and already the lack of routine is affecting me. I scrubbed the shower naked with a toothbrush last night"

"all the noises, the sounds, everything together is making me twitchy. Sensory overload. Touching. Hugging. Arrrggh. Sensory overload"

"had to take a sleeping tablet last night after cutting the hedges down at 9.30pm and getting the urge to gut the cabin and paint it with sparkly paint"

"everyone's voice is pissing me off"

"I wanted to die. I wanted to give up on life. Instead I came home and slept the rest of the day. I hate myself. I never do anything right"

> "I'm getting angry about things that haven't even happened yet"

> "faffing, straightening things up, spotting dirt that's not there, getting angry and anxious over everything"

As you can see, my mood fluctuates a lot. Some of these entries were in just one day during an episode. I had a few diary formats depending on my mood.

If I was low, I would write directly into my notebook. There would be no long sentences but short sharp statements such as 'I want to die'.

If I was hypermanic I wouldn't be able to wait for the notebook. I would type them into an email using my phone wherever I was. If I didn't get those thoughts down, they would be forgotten, and I would get cross later on for not remembering. They would be long paragraphs which would be difficult to follow. I would then print these off and stick them into my notebook.

**Either way, my diary became a vital part of my diagnosis and recovery.**

By the end of 2017, I was feeling stronger. Work was feeling good again and I increased my hours.

My medication was sorted, and my moods had started to stabilise.

MS G L WARWICK

I felt strong enough to end my toxic relationship and I went into 2018 ready to get back to living again and not simply existing.

# CHAPTER TEN – THE CATS

So, I mentioned earlier on about the cats. I've never really enjoyed having pets. We had a cat, rabbits, guinea pigs, budgies, fish and hamsters growing up, my sister even had a lobster but as an adult I felt like they were a nuisance and a waste of money. Why would I want an animal living in my house? An animal that needed feeding, an animal that left fur all over the place and an animal who ruined my carpets. An animal that would need caring for if I went away.

However, the kids wore me down and as I previously mentioned we ended up getting not one but two kittens. We called them Ollie & Poppy. One condition I gave the kids was they had to give them normal names. They were both black and had been born in July 2016 and they eventually made themselves very much at home. Even I could admit they were super cute.

Little did I know at the time, but they would actually become a vital part of my recovery. Having them around me comforted me. They made me feel calm. They made me feel less lonely. They made me feel safe.

> ***"A cat purring on your lap is more healing than any drug in the world, as the vibrations you are receiving are of pure love and contentment"***

The following year (Spring 2017) I felt like I needed some more so, along came Iris and Lily. They were also black and very different to the older two. Again, they quite soon became part of the family. When I picked them up, they were living in a caravan in someone's front garden and that made me very sad. They took a while to settle as they hadn't really been around people before.

In February 2018 we found out that Iris was pregnant. We decided to let the pregnancy play out and, on the 19th April, just three days after my Gran passed away, she gave birth to four healthy little kittens. They were born in a box next to my bed. I rubbed Iris's back as she laboured but I must have fallen asleep because I woke up a couple of hours later to her cleaning her last kitten. It was magical, and a little bit disgusting too! As I write this Iris, now almost three, is snuggled up next to me.

She had three girls who we called Beryl, Violet, Mavis and a boy we called Norman. All named after grandparents. They were adorable and lots of fun but at ten weeks old they were all ready for their new homes. Norman went first and it was quite emotional watching him go. The next was

Mavis. She was gorgeous. She is now called Lola. Norman kept his name though which made me happy. His new owner liked the unique name and decided to keep it. Violet was the last to go. She was very fluffy and very sweet.

So, we were left with just one, **Beryl.**

After much deliberation, I decided to keep her. She was named after my Gran and I didn't feel like I could let her go. She's quite a character and very fluffy. She still is! I call her my little lion.

In Spring 2019 we found out that Violet had given birth to 3 male kittens and as I was now collecting cats I ended up having one. We called him Eric. As I write this, he is 9 months old and a total nut case. We love him lots though.

I didn't want cats. I didn't want hair shedding and carpet scratching animals in my home. I didn't want pets that took all my money and got in the way, but they are now a huge part of our family. I became the crazy cat lady with 6 feline friends within the space of a couple of years and love having them around me. I wouldn't change them for the world now.

As a side note I should add that true to my nature they are all colour coordinated. Red Poppy, Pink Lily and Purple Iris. Green (Olive) Ollie. Beryl is Yellow because that was my Grans favourite colour and Eric is Blue because that was the only colour left and of course he is a boy. Gender stereotype I know!

# CHAPTER ELEVEN - THE HAPPY EVERY AFTER - 2018

New year, new start.

> *"After the rain there's a rainbow*
> *After a storm there's calm*
> *After the night there's a morning*
> *And after an end there is a new beginning"*

After ER left (well was asked to leave) at the end of 2017, I felt liberated and didn't look back.

True to form though, I couldn't be alone and found someone fairly soon afterwards and the excitement was well, exciting! The relationship moved very fast and before I knew it, we had moved his daughter in with us and he gradually moved in unofficially, too. His daughter was 9 years old and just 3 weeks younger than OC. Initially they got on very well and their very obvious differences actually complimented each other.

The first 6 months were perfect, and I was very much caught up in the love and attention and loved how different it felt compared to my time with ER. We camped, we had a romantic weekend away, we planned our 2019 holiday, we laughed, cried and giggled. We welcomed the kitten's courtesy of Iris into the family and we simply tried to make lots of memories as a 'blended family' of five.

Of course, the relationship and the new family dynamics weren't without their issues and by the summer, cracks had started to show. The once happy relationship between OC and AR started to dwindle. AR started to play up. She demanded attention and would gain this by making herself out to be a victim of HC's boyish behaviour. Jealously started to rear its ugly head and she was never happy. It took a strain on both me and the kids but somehow, I managed to stay stable.

Every weekend I prayed that this would be the breakthrough weekend. The weekend where we would have cracked it and things would from now on be different. However, it never was.

I began to resent her and dreaded her coming and so did the kids. However, despite their own feelings of dread they welcomed her with no judgement and a clean slate **every time.** They forgot the previous weekend and never held a grudge. They always gave her the benefit of the doubt and would accept that she was 'tired', 'poorly', 'missing mummy' and so on and so on. For me, they wanted it work and they also tried everything to make her happy.

It was now the summer; we had been together for

6 months and it had been a while since I had had a full-blown episode. I had been stable for at least eighteen months by this point, but I had got flippant with my own self-care and I ended up triggering. I had got pretty good at recognising when I might tip over but this time round, I completely missed it. I was so absorbed in the AR stuff that I started to neglect myself and completely missed the start of an episode.

It started around the beginning of June and I had actually taken a day off in the hope that a day to myself would avoid it getting worse but by the end of the day I was a wreck and super hypermanic.

On the Saturday, MR went sailing whilst I had all 3 children and I didn't sit still all day. If it was stationary, I cleaned it. If it moved, I got angry it was making a mess, that included the cats!

The following day we went to MRs house to get it ready for some tenants to move in. Since MR was hardly there, he moved his stuff into the small room, and I attacked his house and got it ready to rent the bigger rooms out. I saw every speck of dirt. If there was a crease in the cushions it bothered me and a footprint on the freshly hoovered carpet made my blood boil.

When we returned back home, AR put on her swimming costume on and wanted to have a water fight. I asked her not to because it was getting late and I could see the mess (wet floors!) it would create and no doubt an argument would break out when HC squirted water at her in the wrong way, but she ignored me and MR let it happen. It was like he was scared to say no to her. Of course, the inevitable happened and I was the one who was left to clean up the mess and discipline HC. I snapped at MR. I was angry. She got away with everything.

The next day, I fell apart. I was the real definition of a manic depressive. I was a crying wreck with a huge amount of angry irritable energy. I called the doctor and she signed me off for a week. I spent the week cleaning constantly and I threw myself into making bags, purses and all sorts! I made quite a large stock with big plans on how to sell it. **I was invincible and I just kept on going**.

As the week came to an end, my mood was starting to drop. Nevertheless, I was keen to get back to work. I spent the next week with both headphones in. Colleagues asked if I was ok and I really believed I was. I lasted the week and even the start of the following week but by the Wednesday I was in a full depressive state. I cried in silence at my desk. I wanted to go home but attempted to last another week. Thursday was the breaking point. I couldn't handle the noise, the disruption and the silly questions anymore. I walked into my bosses' room and just broke down. She sent me home.

I stayed in bed pretty much for the next 5 days. I

watched The Greatest Showman on repeat – a true sign I wasn't well. Not the choice of film but the fact I was watching it on repeat. I had no desire to change the movie or even the energy and brain power to choose another. Suddenly housework didn't seem important and I would drop HC at school at the last minute so I didn't have to speak to anyone. I isolated myself and ate crap food. I wasn't suicidal but I would have quite happily not been here. I found myself crying for no reason. It was frustrating as I had literally nothing to be sad about.

It did, however, reinforce my diagnosis.

After 9 days off work I started to feel better and literally overnight the depression lifted, and I spent the last few days of my time signed off sick picking up the pieces from the last month.

After a week back at work it was like it had never happened. I was back to my normal self.

> **"Bipolar is a mood system that functions like the weather. Its independent of the things that happen in your life. Sometimes it hits me out of nowhere, all of a sudden this overwhelming sadness rushes over me"**

The rest of year was fairly uneventful from a mental health point of view but there were even more cracks starting to appear in mine & MRs relationship due to the issues with his daughter. Like the fool I am, I chose to ignore them and believed that over time things would get better. His mum and sister kept telling me that so it must have been true, and I did appreciate their optimism.

Despite all the issues, I continued to try my hardest to make her and MR happy. In order to make sure she didn't feel left out I used my own birthday and Christmas money to add to her spending money for our trip in April 2019 and I purchased her Christmas gifts, so she had the same things as my two for holiday. I was trying to avoid a mid-air tantrum or a 12000 mile away meltdown when she realised she didn't have a new towel or new colouring pencils or even worse, only 2 new pairs of socks instead of 3! I wish I could say it was appreciated but it wasn't.

Again, I ignored this and made excuses for her.

I would like to point out that MR wasn't happy to share his own Christmas money and I never got a thank you for sharing mine! Infact he rarely put his hand in his pocket. I paid for everything. I would treat his daughter all the time, but he never got my two anything. I would feed them and make sure she never went without and this was ALWAYS at my expense. Even when we went out for ice-cream with AR's mother in the attempt to show some kind of solidarity, I was the one who ended up buying the food. When we split up, he said to me "you can't buy love" which is true, but I wasn't buying her love. I was doing everything I could to make sure we didn't have a sulking nine-year-old and a stressful weekend. I had no choice but to buy her the same things as my two given the couple of times I didn't we had tears, tantrums and her mum on the doorstep. In the end it was easier to just not get my two anything, but this wasn't teaching her anything really, but it was the quietest and least stressful option and the option that I believed would keep me the most stable. A happy child meant less stress which meant less chance of triggering.

Despite the cracks 2018 ended fairly well. We had a nice Christmas and we saw the new year in as a family of 5 with a renewed hope for 2019.

# CHAPTER TWELVE - THE END OF THE HAPPY EVERY AFTER - 2019

*"Today is the day my life begins…"*
*Alex Karev, Grey's Anatomy*

The year 2019 was supposed to be the year my life began again. The year where only good things were going to happen. I could dream right??!

It started off relatively well, but unfortunately, I triggered at the end of January. I seemed to miss the hypermanic period – I know I had one as I hurt my back from excessive cleaning, but I just don't remember it and as I didn't seem to document any of it, I have no memory of it happening.

Memory issues during a hypermanic period are actually quite common and definitely a symptom I suffer from. Some studies have shown that memory and cognition problems are at their worst during manic episodes. Patients operating at high speeds due to mania have a hard time encoding new information into their memories and also show difficulty accessing memories.

I do, however, remember the low.

I remember wishing I was dead. I didn't want to continue living. I felt unmotivated to care about anything. We had our holiday in April to look forward to, but I wasn't looking forward to it at all. I was scared about what it would do to me mentally. My heart would pound at the thought of leaving my house let alone travelling for 3 weeks with 3 children. Even my boss raised her concerns about what the trip would do to me mentally. I decided to risk it though. I didn't want my illness to ruin everything.

> **"Your illness shouldn't stop you from taking a trip. But it does need to be the first thing you think about. From the initial planning to packing, traveling and returning home, your bipolar disorder will play a key role in every decision that is made"**

I sat in bed all day and I started to doubt my current life choices. Did I rush with MR? Why does everything I touch turn to crap? I want to work but I don't want to work. Why is my mental health always called into question? Why should I be accountable for my motherly actions to everyone? Maybe I should have been alone for a while before rushing into something new? Are people upset with me at work? Do they even believe me? Am I'm a shit mum? Why do I have to look past AR's flaws, but MR is more than keen to keep me apprised with

OC and HCs indiscretions.

I was terrified about Australia. I was worried about my back, my brain, the constant crying from AR, HC being hard work and no doubt my two getting the blame for everything. Were we stupid for attempting to fit so much into 3 weeks?

You will find out later on in this chapter!

<u>Thankfully,</u> my mood lifted in time and I started to get excited at long last. I couldn't wait to go and make memories. I couldn't wait to give my children an amazing holiday and show them more of the world. They already had Chinese stamps in their passports, and they were looking forward to adding more.

The reason for our trip down under was because my youngest sister had recently moved to Perth and was getting married. We decided that we would all go and make it extra special with a stopover in Malaysia and Singapore. A whistle stop tour of where I spent a year and then an even shorter stop in one of favourite places.

I asked earlier "were we mad to have decided to do so much on our holiday?" and I said I would let you know later in the chapter well the answer is …… yes but also no!

Hang on tight and I will explain….

We left for our big adventure on Wednesday 3$^{rd}$

April 2019. We were packed and ready to go. We had 3 excited children and 2 nervous adults hoping that the 2 flights, 13 hours of flying and overall a 24-hour journey would be fairly stress free. Thankfully it was quite easy, the kids were angels and we arrived in Penang in the morning and we headed to our apartment after picking up the rental car at the airport. Penang was where I had lived during the year abroad and we chose to stay quite close to the central tourist bits. We were perfectly situated for our 5 day stay and I for one was super excited to be there.

We managed to visit quite a few places during the time we were there. We went up Penang Hill, we met up with my old friends (and the kids made new ones), we went to the night market and we swam in the apartment blocks private pool. We visited the Botanical Gardens and we ate very well. We went on a hike through the national park and visited turtle beach. I took the kids to one of my favourite places – little India and we had a ride on a trishaw. It was a busy few days.

I did however have waves of sadness. I am one of those people who will smell something familiar and I am instantly transported back to the time in my life I first smelt it. The smells in Penang stirred up some emotions. I had imagined one day MC and I would take the kids together to visit and it made me feel a little sad. None-the-less, I loved showing the kids where I had lived, and it was a magical few days.

That's if you forget about the arguing, the sulking and the four major dramas over sunglasses, balloons and fans in the first five days!

The next stop was Singapore. Just a 48 hour stop en-route to Oz, but we managed the zoo, the luge and the cable car. We also managed a dinner catch up with another friend I had met during my time in Penang who now lives in Singapore with her husband, her daughter and two sons.

After Singapore, we left for our final destination. Australia. The main event so to speak. We arrived late at night and we were met by my dad & stepmother who we then followed in our hire car to our home for the next 10 days.

We all crashed and woke up the next day ready to start to explore Perth and catch up with my sister.

The trip here started off reasonably well. The kids (mine) and I were certainly excited to finally be in Australia. It was quite overwhelming to think we were actually there after all the saving, planning and the detour and journey to get there.

On our first day we went to Caversham wildlife park where we cuddled koalas and fed kangaroos. This was a magical day. This was OC's wish. She had been waiting all year for this day. I loved seeing the excitement in her face. It was a very special day.

They had all picked things that they wanted to do when we were away. I had printed off lots of suggestions a few months before. They were told they could choose two things each and we would make sure that happened for them all. OC had chosen Caversham Wildlife Park and The Cat Café, both in Perth. She was lucky that we also found a cat sanctuary in Penang and so we had an afternoon there as a bonus.

AR chose the aquarium in Singapore and Penguin Island in Perth. HC was quite simple and chose just one thing. He chose the luge in Singapore.

I chose Singapore Zoo and MR chose to visit the filming place of a YouTube video just outside Perth. Everyone got their wishes.

The rest of the trip was fun but also turbulent at times. The kids couldn't handle being in the car together for long and they would get tired from the long days out. At times it was quite stressful, and I did lose my patience regularly. HC was quite a challenge at bedtimes, he would be overtired and wanted me to sit with him like MR did with AR when all I wanted was for him to go and settle down so I could have a few moments to myself. **A vital element in keeping my disorder at bay.**

Despite all of this we managed to visit central Perth, enjoy a hen & stag do and be part of my sister's special day. We went on a road trip to a discovery centre and we went to a very cool science centre which the kids loved. We went to the Cat Café, saw dolphins in the wild (well one dolphin), we went on a boat to Penguin Island and visited the beach a couple of times.

Overall, the three weeks were full of various emotions. We had good days, amazing days, long days, stressful days and crazy busy days. We laughed, made amazing memories, argued, explored and overall, we did have a good time. When it was time to come home, I cried. Despite the downs I had really fallen in love with Australia, as had the kids. OC has decided she is going to live there when she's older and I believe she will. I really hope I get to visit again because it was a beautiful place and I would live there in a heartbeat.

The cracks were even bigger than before though and whilst I didn't admit this at the time, I now realise I had been having doubts about the future of us as a family but forever the optimist I believed it would get better on our return.

When we got home the plan was to sell MRs house and we would officially move into together and generally continue our life as a couple and blended family.

Little did I know that this was to come crashing down at the start of May.

We had been home for just 2 weeks, when I came

home from work one day to discover some of MRs stuff missing. As I searched the house I realised he had cleared everything except his fish tank, furniture and AR's stuff. He had even taken his dirty laundry! He had gone to his mother's house for the evening with OC and AR, so I called him to investigate what was going on. My heart was pounding as I asked the question "are you leaving me?". I was expecting a 'don't be daft' kind of reply but when he responded with "sorry, yes". To say I was shocked, was an understatement. He refused to discuss it on the phone and told me to wait!

HC was out too at his sports club and so I went for the wine. By the time everyone had arrived home (including MR) I had consumed more than a bottles worth of wine and was still going. I think overall, I drank two bottles of wine that evening and I was inconsolable. MR had to put the kids to bed for me and then we sat down to work out what had happened. He wasn't happy apparently – HE WASN'T HAPPY! No care or recognition for the fact that we were all affected by the AR situation. It was all about him. I guess we know where AR gets it from now. He told me he didn't like HC. Ouch. That hurt. He wasn't the easiest child I know, but I was more than happy to admit this. I don't think he even liked OC as he didn't have anything nice to say about her either but most of the conversation was around him not liking HC. I still maintained I loved AR though as I will always look for the best in people and I believed I did love her.

I was eventually more honest with my feelings later on in the month as our promised friendship started to fade.

Feeling hurt, angry, upset, shocked and downright disappointed I decided that alcohol wasn't enough to numb the pain and I started on my tablets. I emptied my dosette boxes onto the bed and started taking them in handfuls. When these were confiscated, I started on the Calpol bottles in the bathroom and even a bottle of cough syrup. I was eventually put to bed by my mother who MR had called for help. She tried to insist on taking me to hospital, but I resisted, and they let me sleep it off.

When I woke the next day, I was glad it was my day off because I was feeling very broken. Both physically from the overdose (which I read later on that day was probably toxic and the pain that spread through my body indicated that that was the case) and I was emotionally broken too. I looked like I had been crying all week not just one night. I had no inclination anything was wrong, and I was still very much in shock. I was hurt because he had obviously been thinking about it for a while and had clearly made plans for this to happen. I had no idea and it was completely out of the blue.

After speaking to his mum, the next day, I was told that my bipolar disorder didn't help, and I shouldn't blame him for finding this hard. I pointed out to her that I had been honest with my disorder from early on in the relationship and he was more than happy to continue with 'us' after he had done his research. I wanted to ask her though, if it had been a physical illness as opposed to a mental health illness would she have been saying that was the reason? I hate the mental health stigma.

> *"I hate it when I tell someone I have bipolar and I see the look of terror in their eyes".*

What started off as hurt, upset and broken hearted turned to anger and outrage. The trip down under was tainted. Every picture a reminder. I have a handful of photographs of just my two and just two photos of me with my two. As stupid as this sounds, I was angry and upset that I hadn't known. He made sure he had plenty of pictures of just AR and pictures of the two of them. Afterall, he had known his intentions before the holiday. This is the one thing that still makes me angry even now. A massive holiday and they are in every memory. I have learnt the hard way with this though and I will never let this happen again. No matter the circumstances, no matter how much I may be trying to include someone into our family I will always make sure I get photos of myself and my two children and make memories just us three. We will make lots of them.

I was heartbroken. I genuinely didn't know where

to start. He basically lived with me. I don't think he realised how much stuff he had at mine, how much our lives were entwined and how concrete lots of our plans were until he started to move his stuff out. I asked him to remove the remainder of his stuff sooner rather than later and also whilst I wasn't there. If he was going, I wanted him gone now. I wanted to get my life and the kids' life back to normal. OC had given up her room for AR to have her own bed and space for her things. With that gone, her room would look empty and I didn't want to waste any time getting her room back to the way it was. We sold her high sleeper (which we had got to make room for AR), and she chose a beautiful day bed from gumtree and we got her room back. I got the house back. That was actually quite liberating.

We stayed friends at the beginning but when I found out he was dating again I decided I needed to break from him. He had told me he didn't want to be with anyone and just wanted to concentrate on AR and his dreams – his boats, his van and getting his property business off the ground and to know he was dating again felt like I had been stabbed in the heart. I decided I needed no contact, nothing. A complete break. This was a hard decision and I do often think of him, but I know it was the right thing to do.

I said previously that I was eventually honest with how I felt about the whole situation. Anger was boiling inside me and I told him how I felt. How I was made to feel. I told him that I was angry about the holiday pictures. I told him he made me feel like an idiot. I told him I couldn't have him in my life anymore. I told him I thought she was a brat and will never change if she is allowed to get away with it. I told him how I felt the amount of exaggeration and sneaky behaviour she used with my two was ridiculous.

I wished him luck and told him she is going to be one spoilt entitled little brat when she is older.

**"Children need to learn to take responsibility for their actions, so they do not become adults believing that nothing is ever their fault"**

As soon as I hit send, I collapsed in a panic attack and lots of tears and struggling to breathe followed. I couldn't believe I had just text all of that, but it was actually quite therapeutic and once I had got it all out of my system, I felt much better and ready to move on and put it all behind me.

The time between May and September were fun, stressful and emotional. I went on lots of dates, made mistakes and got things out of my system. At the end of September, I went on a date with CW. This was just after another depressive period.

We took it slowly. We only saw each other a couple of times a week. Usually once in the week and then at the weekends. He is grown up and yet silly too.

He wasn't my usual type, but I liked that. We only ended up seeing each other for a few months but I enjoyed our time together.

Despite the setbacks, 2019 wasn't so bad in the end. Our holiday was stressful, but we cuddled koalas, stroked cats at the cat café & Penang cat sanctuary, fed kangaroos and my little sister got married. The children had added three new stamps to their passports and became the envy of all their friends.

We did only manage one camping trip which was disappointing as I usually like to do a few more weekends than that but it was with my best friends and it was amazing.

We had purple hair. We baked and did lots of crafts. I got four new tattoos.

We got another kitten and HC was selected for a junior athletics club and is now excelling there.

OC had her usual above average school report and my mum turned 60. I managed to pull off another 2 great birthday parties for the kids, and I finished the year with renewed optimism.

I also managed to keep my 2018 New Year's resolution to read more and I managed to read 35 books.

Oh and my nephew LA, who lives in China, was here for Christmas. That was quite special.

# CHAPTER THIRTEEN – MANAGING MY MOOD

***"Even when I am really great, steady and stable – I am clinically bipolar, so a darkness always exists"***

So let's talk about triggers.

These are different for everyone but for me the two main triggers are tiredness and lack of routine. I find school holidays are the biggest trigger. No longer am I dropping the children to school, going to work and leaving at 3pm to collect them. I will instead be dropping them at my parents, my sisters, sports clubs, a friend's or they will be with their dad. Every day is different, and this lack of routine is a huge trigger waiting to happen.

The other is the later nights, the long days out with them on my days off and so on and so on. Historically the two most common times I've triggered are Jan, after the christmas holidays and Sept after the summer holidays. I seem to be ok after Easter for some reason though! Quite possibly because the weather is typically nicer and its usually too hot to hide away.

The hardest bit of having bipolar however, isn't the episodes themselves, it's the determination to not trigger into an episode in the first place. The medication ritual, the strict routine and the often-antisocial behaviour such as cancelling plans when I just know I'll end up tired and overwhelmed. I do often feel trapped and left unable to be overly spontaneous, but I know it's vital in order to stay stable.

If I can feel my mood changing, I steer myself into a different direction. I listen to music at work to block out the keyboard tapping and the chatter, I avoid alcohol and if I find myself struggling to sleep, I will take sleeping tablets to help with this. If I manage to get decent sleep, then an episode is less likely.

If my mind is easily distracted, then I make lists and write things down. Lists are really important to me and I do operate better with one, but they tend to just include relevant things now rather than 'the perfect pink cushion' amongst other things. I think currently my list says 'fix toilet, sort shed roof, get flea treatments for the cats' – fairly normal items to be on a to-do list! I also like a spreadsheet too and a nice diary outlook – mainly for the school holidays. I refuse to go completely online, as I need a printout for visual purposes.

**These are all coping mechanisms and ways to manage my mood.**

I avoid late nights, at least until the triggering feeling passes. Most importantly I have learnt over the last few years to rest when I know I have a long day ahead or have had a busy few days. I have learnt to attempt to keep some form of routine.

**"Self-care rule: don't say yes to others if it means saying no to your wellness. If you don't pick a day to relax, your body will pick it for you"**

However, this isn't fool proof. It has been a learning curve and with every episode they usually come out of nowhere no matter how hard I try to avoid them. That's the thing about bipolar – everything can be going very well and out of nowhere I will spiral into an episode.

A common issue with bipolar disorder is feeling better. I know that sounds completely crazy but when I start to feel better, I start to increase my workload, I will go out more and I will make more plans. If I do too much though I trigger. I am also more likely to mess up my meds as I will be out more, and I get the attitude 'it won't matter if I miss one dose'. Silly, silly G!

So, at what point does being stable become the evil. If I am stable, I am not living my full life. I am just existing. I sometimes wonder if it might be easier if I just trigger a few times a year

*Extract from a psychiatrist letter, January 2018*
*– "G had 3 days off her medication by mistake as*

> *she was away from home. This led to a marked deterioration in her mental health. This reinforced her understanding that she needs to stick with her present medication"*

I recently changed how the childcare was divided up between MC and I. We did alternate weeks where we would either have the kids all weekend or we would have all weekend to ourselves, but I found this quite tough. It was all or nothing. I found both weekends long for different reasons. A whole weekend with them was tough but then a weekend without them was actually quite boring so we now do one day of the weekend each. This changes each week. One week we have them Friday night to Sunday morning then they will go to the other one of us late morning on the Sunday and overnight and then vice versa. It's been a few months now and it seems to be working. I appreciate the break once a week rather than every fortnight. I think it suits MC too.

All the changes of course do not guarantee stability though and I will continue to find new ways as time goes on to manage my disorder.

This is getting easier as the kids get older as they pick up on the signs - my daughter, often before me - and they will help me to avoid triggering. No matter how annoying my children are I am lucky to have them. OC is pretty grown up for her age and recognises when I need a little help and HC is kind and sensitive beneath his crazy boyish ways.

I am still hopeful for a fulfilling life whilst staying stable.

# CHAPTER FOURTEEN – THE CHILDREN

The children are amazing when I am poorly but naturally, it does affect them. They don't know if they will get the mummy who will make a roast or the mummy who tells them to help themselves to whatever they want from the cupboard or the mummy who can't even stand being around them.

They don't know if they are getting the mummy who insists on routine and the one who gets angry when they make a mess or if they are getting the mummy who encourages the mess!

I am very good at arranging things and promising to take them places but, when the time comes around, I am usually unable to fulfil these promises because my good sociable mood has subsided. It kills me to write that.

It breaks my heart that I treat them like that, but I can't control it. I know at times I am quite frankly a rubbish mother and I worry that it will affect them long term.

I am pretty good at hiding most of it though and with the exception of staying in bed a lot they don't usually notice my major incidents but in May 2019 they witnessed my attempted overdose. They had never seen me that bad as I usually save those moments for when they aren't with me.

That was the day that I found out that my relationship with MR was over and I drank almost a box of wine, took as many tablets as I could get in my mouth, I drank the contents of 3 Calpol bottles and a bottle of cough syrup.

MR had called my mother and my sister to help. My sister put the children back to bed, my mother put me to bed and comforted me (those who know me well will know that I do not like cuddles with my mother!!) and MR looked upon helplessly knowing his spineless way of 'telling' me it was over had caused this. Anyone with or without a mental health disorder would have reacted negatively in some way at discovering their partner had cleared their stuff out when they weren't there.

Unfortunately, the children witnessed all of this. The next day I was ashamed that I had exposed them to this, but I believed they hadn't noticed too much overall as my sister attempted to shelter them for and from me.

It wasn't until the start of 2020 when I came down with a sickness bug that I realised how much it had affected HC. He had gone to his dads for the night, which I was very grateful for given how poorly I was feeling. Apparently, he suddenly flipped and wanted to come home. He couldn't explain why, but he walked out of his dad's house and began his journey to my house on foot (thankfully just around the corner). His dad found him and brought him home. HC sobbed and I finally got out of him what his concerns were. Through tears he was able to tell me that the last time I was 'poorly' he watched me (yes I know, I know) take too many tablets (don't worry, I wasn't alone, see previous paragraph) and he associated 'poorly' with my being poorly this time. Of course the difference in the illnesses were the one in May was mental health related and the one in January was a sickness bug but to a very sensitive eight year old boy, poorly, simply meant poorly and he was worried if I was left alone this time when I was poorly that I would do the same as last time.

This broke my heart into a million pieces but then equally, I was very proud of him. He had recognised I needed some help and wanted to keep me safe. He may be a little monkey at times, but I am raising quite a caring and thoughtful little man and he makes me smile. Sometimes anyway!

I am actually quite proud of them both. Whilst I have been going on about how the last few years have affected me; I am aware the last few years would have affected them too. They have dealt with a house fire, the divorce of their parents, the turbulent relationship I had with ER, the MR and AR stuff and of course my breakdown, the diagnosis and all that led up to that and the fact that at times I really can be a very shit mother. They have had quite a lot to deal with in their short life.

Despite all of this, I am managing to raise two incredible tiny humans. HC doesn't like the academic side of school, but he isn't behind and I'm happy enough with that. His strengths are in his sports. His running speed is phenomenal for an eight-year-old doing an off-road park in just 25 minutes and he attends many after school clubs as well as an athletics club.

OC is the total opposite. She is my genius. She LOVES school and this shows in her grades. Her teachers love her, and she is very popular amongst her peers. At her last parents evening the teacher asked if she could photocopy her because she would love a whole class of OC's. She, on the other hand, hates sports but loves sewing, reading and crafting. She loves tests and getting extra homework. She is amazing at looking after me when I am down, and she will check that I have taken my tablets. When she sees my mood has dropped, she instantly clicks into carer mode and will help me with HC. It kills me to write that, but she is awesome, and I am so proud of her.

Overall, I am very proud of both of them. Even if there are times where they drive me insane.

Extracts from their school reports show just how different they are...

*"We love having HC in our class. He is cheeky, full of fun and has a great sense of humour. We are working however, to make sure his comments are well timed and don't cause hilarity at an inappropriate moment".*

He is such a clown, but we love him anyway and it's nice to see his personality shine despite everything he has experienced in short, his life.

*'OC is an absolute pleasure to teach. She is a friendly and polite member of our class and has an exemplary attitude towards her work. She enjoys a breadth of subjects the curriculum offers and has an attention detail, always striving to produce perfection"*

She loves school, she loves learning and is an odd child who loves tests. She is a happy girl who is growing up too quickly for my liking.

Unfortunately, bipolar is hereditary (my youngest sister found out recently that she also has the disorder) and so, naturally I am concerned about my two, particularly OC, as she displays so many of my character traits. She's shy and yet always aims to please. She is emotional and already shows what I would I describe as 'mini' hypermanic moments. She will be on the go and can be found cleaning her room and organising her pencils into colour order late in the evening when I thought she was asleep. She is also very dedicated to challenges and tasks – just as I am. Like me, she also finds confrontation hard and doesn't like to answer questions at school (even though she knows they are right) for the fear of getting them wrong.

I don't really have a fear of her having it as such as for me to 'fear' it would indicate it's a terrible thing to have and this would feed the stigma but, we know what to spot and I now know how to manage it so, if she has it, she has it, but of course I wouldn't want to put anyone through this ideally.

As for HC, he doesn't display any signs of bipolar, but he does have signs of the EUPD and has traits of autism, **in my unprofessional view anyway**. He is obsessed with order and he struggles when out of routine and is very set in his ways. He also really struggles with his emotions. He is a wild child but underneath he is a very sensitive little man and has issues explaining himself when he is sad, upset, worried or has got something wrong and this often results in anger. We are getting better at noticing these traits and we are gradually learning how to cope with them when they occur. He often has meltdowns at school if he can't do something well or if he has forgotten his P.E kit or something. We have managed to narrow down most of his outbursts to worrying about something such as when Eric, the kitten, was at the vets for an operation. He worried all day, and this came out as negative and disruptive behaviour.

I am very grateful to the teachers that have supported him and recognised he isn't being naughty when he acts up but is usually worrying about something and they have worked with him to help him display his frustrations and worries in a less disruptive way. He recently found out his new teacher for next school year and he sobbed. He has spent the last year with a super supportive teacher who has worked with him and he is worried, the thought of change has unsettled him, so I really hope he goes into his next year positively as opposed to the negative feeling he is currently experiencing.

*(Edit June 2021 - his new teacher was amazing with him and he loves her as do we!)*

I really hope that no matter what happens with both of them with regards to their mental health that they tell me when they are down or need some extra help. I will certainly be on high alert.

I briefly mentioned earlier the hereditary factor. According to psychcentral.com "There is no single cause for bipolar disorder. Indeed, like all psychological disorders, bipolar disorder is a complex condition with multiple contributing factors, including genetics. Bipolar disorder tends to run in families, so researchers believe there is a genetic predisposition for the disorder".

My mum has had her own mental health struggles and I believe if she was to have been diagnosed formally, she would also have the same diagnoses as me. I hate to admit it but whilst OC is a lot like me, I am also a lot like my mum! Please do not tell her I said that! She also loves organising her stationary and having late night cleaning along with days in bed feeling low. Of course, this isn't enough to diagnose anyone with bipolar or any other mental health disorders and there is obviously more to her mood changes than I have mentioned above but that would be her own story to tell.

# CHAPTER FIFTEEN - MY DIARIES

I used to write a diary when I was younger. I enjoyed writing them. I found they gave me peace and they were another type of outlet. I also wrote diaries during my time in Penang and during my first pregnancy.

Unfortunately, they have all been lost in transit through my moves over the years so in Sept 2016 I started writing another one. This was just before I started to see the psychiatrist. I kept this going daily for around 2 years and since then I add the odd entry when my mood is at either end of the scale but the general day to day, I don't need to write about much these days.

***Extract from psychiatrist, October 2017** – "G has been completing a very comprehensive mood diary over the last few months. We have found that this has been very helpful in that we have been able to discuss in detail her various moods and triggers"*

I don't read them back very often but when I do, I am still surprised at some of the things I used to write.

The psychiatrist said to me once 'if you ever feel low then look back at old diaries and you will see that it did, and does, get better and the feelings go away eventually'. Thankfully my mood doesn't fluctuate like it used to and as a result I haven't had to look back for a while.

**"The only time you should ever look back is to see how far you have come"**

I thought I would share a diary entry I wrote in 2017 after a hypermanic episode. It is quite a significant entry.

After a week of hypermanic productivity I found myself asking the following questions...

- Did it matter that HC's drawers on his unit didn't match the others?
- Did I really need a new duvet?
- Did I really need to buy all those extra box frames just in case I needed them?
- Did I need to buy new doormats because the old ones didn't go with the new colour scheme!
- Did I need to go to The Range four times and buy an excessive amount of craft supplies?
- Did I need to go to B&M?

The answer is no, no, no I didn't. but in that moment, at that time, it was important for me to do these things.

I simply couldn't have unmatching items in the dining room – what would people think of me?

However,

- Did I need to remember the kid's appointment at the dentist?
- Did I need to make sure the kids were appropriately fed rather than stocking up on easy snacks, so I don't have to make proper food for them?
- Did I need to take the cat to be neutered?
- Should I have paid in the cheques for running club like I promised?
- Should I have been more concerned with Christmas shopping instead of random shopping and new colour schemes?

**The answer is yes, yes, yes, I most certainly did.**

Why was a new shower curtain and having a perfect bedroom more important than all of that? During an episode I have no rational thoughts though and none of this enters my brain when I am hypermanic.

I am glad I wrote my diaries; they are hard to read back sometimes but also very insightful and I would recommend writing a diary to anyone. No matter the format just getting thoughts down on paper can be very therapeutic.

# CHAPTER SIXTEEN – WORK

*"Anyone with a mental health issue has good and bad days, either copes well or struggles but that doesn't mean they aren't responsible, reliable or able to do a very good job" www.timetochange.co.uk*

I started working at the tender age of just 16. I have always worked. I enjoy the challenges work brings, I enjoy learning new things and when I am normal, I enjoy being around people. I love earning my own money and being independent. I feel that on the whole I am a fairly good employee. I am never late. I work hard. I usually go above and beyond what is expected of me and I have been told in the past by several different employers and colleagues that I am very diligent. My biggest strength at work is my organisation skills and my commitment to a task. My personality doesn't allow me to leave a job unfinished.

My most recent role was at a local doctor's surgery. I have worked there as a Clinical Coder since September 2015. For the most part I really enjoyed the job. I am quite literate in medical terminology now and enjoy impressing people with my knowledge!

A Clinical Coder is a health information professional whose main duties are to analyse clinical statements and assign standard codes using a classification system. This means I spent my days reading over clinic letters, discharge summaries and other medical documents and extracting important information from them and adding this information to patients notes and making decisions on whether this information is needed by the doctor or not. I worked out the other day that I have probably read in the region of 70'000 clinic letters since I started working there.

Unfortunately, despite my efforts when I am there my time there has been turbulent from a sickness point of view and I have had big chunks of time signed off sick. **The problem is when I am good, I am really good.** I work hard. I do overtime and I love being there but when I am having an episode the last thing, I can think about is work. If I am hypermanic I can't sit still, I am fidgety, I have no concentration and I often state 'I'm a liability' when I'm in that state. When I am low the thought of getting out of bed and dressed seems like an impossible task.

I have been asked whether work is right for me and would I be better off being unemployed or being self-employed again but I couldn't imagine not working. Work helps me with structure and routine which is vital to my stability. I love the camaraderie in the office, and it gives me a sense of worth. I hate being off work. I need the company and something to occupy my mind. I have to sometimes stop myself from agreeing to do overtime. Whilst I may feel good at the time by over doing it, I could trigger an episode.

**The key is to stay busy but not too busy. This is actually quite hard to achieve.**

According to www.bipolar.org.uk just 21% of people with a long-term mental health condition are in employment. I am proud to be part of these 21% even if at times it is hard work.

After my episode in September 2018 I was given monthly progress meetings. I am told I'm doing well, and they are pleased with my progress. The real conclusion is it's been a mixture of luck and real focus on not getting sick again which is actually incredibly hard work. What I do find a little frustrating about this however is, it often makes me feel like a little child. I feel like I am being watched and my moods scrutinised. I am constantly reminded of my disorder. I appreciate the care and effort but equally I feel that my mental health is always called into question and everything I say or do is because of my Bipolar. Sometimes, maybe, just maybe it's just me and who I am outside of my disorder.

I'm no fun when I'm trying not to trigger. I can't stay up late, I can't have people round, I don't do much overtime, I keep a regular routine. This is all exhausting! It's a catch 22. I love having people over but the next day I'm shattered and tearful and stressing that the house is dirty. It's a viscous circle because if I was on my own, I would be unhappy! Neither option suits my mood disorder!

No wonder I am hard to live with!!

What I do know however, is work is something I definitely have to keep up no matter how hard it gets sometimes. I will become worse without it. I would trigger more being at home all day. Working gives me a purpose. A reason to get up and out of the house in the morning. I would most definitely become extremely suicidal if I didn't work.

*"There are many challenges to having bipolar and keeping a job, but experts say work can actually be quite helpful to people with bipolar disorder. Work can give a sense of structure, reduce depression and increase confidence" Heathonline.com*

So, I choose work. I choose to not let this disorder beat me. I choose to find coping mechanisms as opposed to just giving up.

# CHAPTER SEVENTEEN – OBSESSIONS

I have mentioned obsessions previously (see chapter one). I do not do things by half. I throw my heart and soul into everything I do. Whether it be a task at work, planning a holiday, a hobby or organising an event. **I am all or nothing. I am a completer finisher.**

The psychiatrist once said to me, that an obsession is only clinically diagnosed OCD if it affects your life to the point you are unable to live it to its full potential. Checking the door 10 times before leaving, 18 hours a day cleaning, showering 5 times a day – these are all examples of a true Obsessive-Compulsive Disorder. The term is quite often used flippantly to describe someone who likes to have their house clean, will hoover a couple of times a day and can't leave the house without making the bed. These are all things I do but yet they don't affect my life enough to be classed as OCD.

I love having my house clean and need to have order in my life. My clothes are all on the same hangers and hanging the same way. I can't leave the house or go to bed without tidying the lounge and having the remotes and cushions straight. The kitchen has to be pristine and everything put away. Everything has a home, and everything matches. I have to have clean bedding and I hoover at least twice a day. I clean the kitchen sides and dust more than I probably need to and I worry a little too much about making sure my knickers are folded correctly in my drawers. I also have this thing about symmetry, and everything has to match. **This doesn't mean though that I have obsessive compulsive disorder. This just means I like a clean, tidy and organised house**. I am one of the very few people to wash, dry and put the washing away all in one day!

However, some people with bipolar disorder experience OCD symptoms without having OCD. This is known as having OCD tendencies. They may only experience these symptoms when they have a very low or very high mood. This also describes me.

I will become obsessed with an idea when I am hypermanic. It will take over my life. The cleaning will become more than just cleaning. I will organise rooms, scrub everything within an inch of their lives and can be found at Ikea at random times. If I have a big idea such as my sewing business, reading, work and **even writing this book** I will dedicate every hour available to that project.

It's all a little bit complicated though because I

could start and get obsessed with a project when I am hypermanic **BUT** will continue it through to completion even after my episode has finished which is unusual for a bipolar sufferer, usually the project would be left unfinished.

Such as running. I started running during a low period of time, but this didn't end when my episode did, it carried on for a couple of years and I became obsessed with beating my times and once I had achieved all of my goals I stopped running.

**I guess this is where my actual personality, my emotionally unstable personality disorder and the bipolar disorder all cross over (more on this later).**

Another example is when I started to make some stock for craft shows. I made dozens and dozens of items, I then purchased coat stands, I painted advertising boards, I made posters and price lists. I replenished my fabric collection and I just kept on making. I made a website and spent ages making it perfect. A year later and 75% of that stock was still in the cabin collecting dust. I lost interest once I had done all the preparation and my enthusiasm waned.

Earlier this year I got back into reading. This became an obsession. I purchased over 100 books and would read every minute I had spare. Not a bad obsession overall but I didn't need to buy so many books. I would spend hours researching books, making a wish list on Amazon and finding complete sets. I even got some of the books I read at university (the theorists I used in my dissertation) and loads of other books I had read before.

I have this issue whereby I can't just buy one colour, one theme, one style. If something comes in blue, pink and purple, I'll get one of each. If something comes in the same colour but different styles, I'll have one of each please. Equally I can't buy something for one child if there isn't a matching version for the other one. I am a little weird I know!

*Some of my obsessions don't start during an episode but appear when I am normal.*

*Some of my obsessions trigger an episode.*

*An obsession could happen during an episode.*

*I could have an obsession without an episode.*

*It isn't clear cut.*

At my job at the doctors I started re-doing all our protocols and I went on a mission to get them done. They are all in the same font, format and tried and tested by the team. I went above and beyond to get these done. I even took them home. I didn't stop until I had finished. None of this was during an episode though.

I consider myself quite a rubbish mother at times,

but I always throw a good birthday party or too. Again, I don't do these by halves.

Last year OC's party was a sewing party. We got the sewing machines out, I prepared stuffed animals and their favours were sewing kits with fabric, pins, scissors and much more and naturally they all matched. The day started at 10am and lasted 24 hours. They went in the hot tub, did each other's hair and nail varnish. They ate sweets and plenty of popcorn. The year before we took a few of her friends camping. I am always throwing myself into every fine detail for their parties, almost more than a wedding! The only thing is I set the bar higher each year. It will soon be time to decide on what we are doing for her next birthday. I believe she is contemplating camping again.

A few years ago, I had grand ideas to become some kind of jewellery entrepreneur and we created White Rose Crafts. I loved setting up the paperwork, order forms, poster and lots of stock. I then did the same with childminding. I enjoyed using my experience from the nursery and created my policies and procedures. I ended up enjoying this more than the actual childminding. I seem to get an idea and I have to go with it. It's usually the prep and the paperwork side I love the most of about it. Once I have done that, I lose interest. Again, neither of these were during episodes, but I did get obsessed with the ideas.

During these 'obsessions' it is all I can think about and I don't rest until I can get home from work and get back to working on the latest 'project'. Even writing this book took over my life!

I also use obsessions to hide away. I would do anything to keep me busy from all of my thoughts. Spreadsheets, lists, lots and lots of lists. I need this organisation when I'm low, normal and hypermanic. It's just the level of organisation that changes depending on my mood. My OCD tendencies are definitely heightened when I am hypermanic and reduced when I am depressed. I also have an obsession with stationary, duvet covers, bunting, dresses, fabric and handbags. These obsessions are always there! That is just part of what makes me, me!

# CHAPTER EIGHTEEN – RELATIONSHIPS

*"If you remove all the mistakes of your past, you'd also erase all of the wisdom of your present. Remember the lesson, not the disappointment"*

My bipolar affects both relationships, friendships and how my family percieve me and cope with me. I know I can be quite hard to be around when I am having an episode. I tend to hide away during the low period but during the high period I can be quite snappy and indecisive and angry if someone tries to get in my way.

Equally the wrong kind of relationship, friendship and family support can affect my bipolar and cause me to trigger.

Since MC and I have been separated I have had 2 long term relationships and a more recent one which ended after just a few months.

ER was the first relationship I had. We saw each other for 3 years but he broke me. This relationship was toxic from the beginning but due to my insecurities and my need for an attachment I chose to ignore the signs and let him get away with far too much.

Even though I could see it all at the time I was unable to see it clearly and when I now look back, I can see the relationship was, by no means, healthy for me.

He was very unreliable. He would lie as to where he had been, chose to spend time at the gym or with another woman over seeing me. He started to treat my house like a hotel and would come to see me late at night but would never spend the evening with me. He would get cross if I wasn't awake when he got there. This of course would all compromise my mood stability. **Being woken up late in the evening/early hours of the morning would interrupt my sleep cycle and so and so on.** He wouldn't care though.

He would promise me a weekend together then he would suddenly have to work, and the weekend was ruined. This didn't help my mood in the slightest. The amount of times (with detective work) I found out he wasn't working at all but had chosen to let me down to spend time with another woman. I won't reveal how I found out these things so as to not share my stalker like secrets but....

Understandably I would react to all these disappointments and I would get upset and angry. **The way I dealt with it though wasn't normal.** I would drink, I would become obsessed with finding out where he was, I would get in my car and drive for hours (not after I have been drinking, I might add!) and I would sleep.

I would sleep and cry, sleep and cry.

> **"Never under any circumstances underestimate a woman's ability to find things out. Whatever you did, she will find out"**

He ruined my self-esteem. He made me believe I was a pyscho (what type of significant other does that!) and I let him take me for granted. He was rude to me, didn't respect me or my time, was incredibly selfish and never did anything for me at all. I was deeply unhappy, but I pretended everything was fine. I never met his family; I wasn't allowed to and they didn't even know I existed. He would let me down time and time again. I believed this was my life now and I wouldn't have a real relationship again. It was all I deserved.

I had a friend say to me 'you will meet the one' one day and he will sweep you off your feet'. I struggled to believe this. No one would want me.

Whilst ER was a twat though, had I not met him I wouldn't have taken myself to the doctors and wouldn't have ended up diagnosed. I would quite likely have ended up dead. I appreciate this sounds dramatic, but this was definitely a possibility.

Despite this I wanted us to be over. I guess as harsh

as it sounds, he had served his purpose.

> **"People always walk into your life for a reason. Sometimes they are blessings and other times they are lessons"**

I decided at the end of 2017 to end the relationship and I felt liberated as I watched him leave that last time. The pain however didn't end. That stayed with me. I was already broken.

Unfortunately, I carried this pain and hurt over into my next relationship.

I met MR shortly after I ended things with ER. Initially everything was fine. He was supportive and made sure I knew I could speak to him freely. The kids got on well and everything seemed to be going well. This was until his daughter started to play up. She demanded her daddy's attention, blamed my children for everything and I chose to put my heart and soul into making her happy. This was to the detriment of my own two.

We went on a huge holiday and this was indeed tough at times but with 3 children and 3 countries it wasn't going to be without its flaws.

On our return MR moved his stuff out one day when I was at work. This broke my heart. I had no inclination anything was wrong. I was angry too. He had chosen to take the easiest way out. It felt like all my efforts with his daughter were thrown back in my face. I was extremely hurt by all of this and how our relationship ended.

After MR and I split, I had 5 months of dating. This was actually quite exhausting, but I did have some fun along the way. At several points during this time and even sometimes now, I did think that maybe I should just be single!?

The one thing I do know, though, is that I will always now, struggle with relationships. My trust and my self-esteem are pretty much zero and I don't even know what love is meant to feel like anymore.

ER ruined my trust, broke me down and made me feel worthless. He broke me into a million pieces and I'm not sure I will ever be completely mended from that. MR has ruined my belief in love and I no longer trust my instincts anymore.

I thought I loved both of them, but I now think it was my insecurities that loved them. I thought they both loved me too, but I am now not sure they ever did. They both just loved the attention I gave them, the chances I gave them and how much I looked after them and cared for them. They both loved how I put them on a pedestal and couldn't ever see anything they were doing was wrong.

Throw in the ER, MR and AR stuff and I am always on edge. I am quite convinced my next relationship will be ruined by HC. I often wonder if the issue was HC and not AR all along. I don't think it was. HC could be annoying and wind her up, but it was her reactions to that which always provided the most drama. She could never just shake it off as HC just being 2 years younger and a boy. Despite knowing he wasn't the main cause I can't help but feel that way.

I started dating again before the summer and I did meet a guy and we got on really well. We spoke on the phone every night and were in constant contact with each other. We saw each other a few times and then we slept with each other. The next day he suddenly disappeared and blocked me. He would then unblock me and apologise. This went back and forward for a couple of weeks. We saw each other a few more times but each time would end the same way. Turns out he was simply adding notches to his bedpost after a 25-year relationship.

This all threw my confidence quite a lot. I thought he liked me. I now, don't know if the connection was real or if he was faking it. It did mess me up.

I mentioned in chapter 12 that I met CW in Sept 2019. I almost didn't go on my date with him because I was still a little muddled about it all and I didn't trust my instincts anymore but after one cancelled date (nerves to be dating again so I cancelled) and the fact he was the one who asked to rearrange I decided to go. We went for lunch and it was a lovely first date but to be honest I didn't expect to hear from him again. **He's way out of my**

**league**, but we kept on seeing each other and over the course of a few weeks made the commitment to be 'boyfriend and girlfriend'. Such a youthful term I know but I don't like the alternatives such as partner, significant other and other half, in my opinion they all sound pretentious and don't really explain the part of a relationship we are in. I feel they all relate to couples living together but unmarried. So, we went with boyfriend and girlfriend. Unfortunately, we ended at the start of 2020.

The situation in the summer affected me more than I realised because whenever CW didn't respond for hours and then eventually did, I would cautiously open the text expecting it to be a 'it's over' message and to then find I've been blocked. I knew he was more mature than that but that's what my low self-esteem does to me.

If he didn't kiss me or want to have sex, I instantly thought the worst. If he didn't hold my hand, I would think it's because he didn't want to be seen with me. If he didn't instigate seeing me then I panicked that he didn't want to see me. If he didn't text me at night, as irrational as it sounds, I found this unsettling (my mind instantly thought it was because he was too busy to think about me) and I didn't sleep very well.

I do know that my low self-esteem was something he struggled to understand. I was torn between showing him my vulnerability but probably scaring him off or hiding my fears but him believing everything is fine. I think I quite possibly scared him off!

I know my family also struggle when I am in the middle of an episode. On the whole I do tend to keep myself to myself most of the time these days anyway. Too much family time, rather harshly, is a trigger. Sorry mum!

As for my friends. I don't have many and I like it that way. The few I do I choose to have in my life though are amazing. They understand and are always checking on me. We don't see each other very often these days but when we do it's like we saw each other yesterday and I am very grateful for their friendship.

> *"Friends are the family we choose." Meredith Grey, Grey's Anatomy*

When I was doing a first proofread on my finished piece, I realised I didn't have many nice things to say about ER and MR. Ultimately this was because I was focusing on the bad parts and the way they made me feel and how they affected my daily struggles with my mental health. There were nice parts too though.

MR was kind, caring, he hugged me lots and always told me he loved me. He would go out of his way to show me he cared about me. If we didn't see each other he would call me. We had some lovely days out, sleepovers in his van at the sailing club, we would cook dinner together and generally had a lovely relationship just us two. Most of the negative was linked to the children and the blended family element and not about us two as a couple.

ER was the total opposite to MR. He wasn't overly caring and didn't give me much concern, but he was generous. He paid for everything when we went out and would throw money at me to treat myself to all sorts. He had this thing about buying me 'frocks'. He would pay for our weekends away and I've acquired some nice camping gear because he bought stuff randomly and ended up leaving it at mine.

As I write this, I am currently single and in no rush to meet anyone. Before I make a commitment again, I want to make sure it's real.

# CHAPTER NINETEEN
# – MARRIAGE

I haven't really discussed my relationship and marriage with MC as yet. I've mentioned that we met in 2003. I have told you when we got our first house and about our year abroad. You know we had two children and that we had a house fire. What I haven't told you is why our marriage broke down.

The first five years were good (with the exception of his dad passing away). There was university, our new house and work was going well for both of us. We had our year abroad and we planned our wedding. Life was good and so was our relationship. There were days where we hated each other of course. We wouldn't be human if we didn't argue on occasion.

OC came along a few months before our first wedding anniversary (and our 6$^{th}$ together) and everything carried on as normal. We moved to a new house in April 2010 when OC was 9 months old and by the October, we were expecting HC.

Once he was born everything changed. HC was

quite a handful as a baby and then even more as a toddler. I was lucky enough by this point to not need to work as financially we could afford for me to be a stay at home mother. This sounded quite appealing to begin with but being at home with two tiny humans all day was actually quite lonely. I would look forward to MC arriving home from work. I wanted us to sit down of an evening, eat together and discuss our days but he would go running, shower and then sit and watch the TV (usually a programme I was not interested in) and so I would go upstairs and spend the evening on my own. I would then wait for him to come to bed so we could lie there talking then instead but he would always come to bed late and by this point I was usually asleep.

We started to grow apart. I was lonely. I started to resent him for having a life outside the home. My self-esteem plummeted due to the lack of attention and affection I received from him. We never cuddled or kissed.

In 2013 we 'celebrated' our 10$^{th}$ anniversary together and my sister offered to have the children for a few days so could go away and celebrate. We chose to go to Dubai. It was a beautiful hotel on the beach.

The weekend, whilst it was beautiful, warm and sunny it showed how many cracks were in our marriage. Our romantic weekend away was filled with time in the sports bar and the gym and this wasn't what I had in mind at all. During the daytimes he would lay there with his iPod playing in his ears whilst reading a book. We barely exchanged a word to each other except at mealtimes. When we returned home, I was devastated about how our weekend had gone.

Life then simply returned to normal.

In the evenings I would hide away upstairs on my own. I would cry during the day and make sure the house was clean for when he got home. I was simply a cleaner and a mother and because of this I started to really resent the children. I was seriously unhappy, but I wasn't sure what to do for the best. I had always maintained that my children would not come from a broken home but by the following September I couldn't lie to myself anymore and I made the very quick decision to end things. I had originally planned to go to the doctor around this time as naturally my mood was very low, but he convinced me otherwise.

When I was diagnosed a year later with bipolar, his whole attitude changed, and he is quite supportive now and will often watch out for an episode. His whole attitude towards mental health in general is now very different and when I am feeling low, he recognises that I may need a little more help with the children during those times.

All in all, we were together 11 years plus the year

we had to live together because of the house fire.

Do I regret leaving him?

Sometimes a wave of regret will come over me when HC announces he misses him (like when he drew a picture of the family and it was us four) but overall no. We weren't meant to be. We were meant to have children together (we did make a couple of good ones) but we weren't meant to last forever.

I have been asked by a few people as to whether I would get married again. When MC and I separated I made the very bold statement that I wouldn't want to live with another boy, merge finances or indeed get married again. I wanted to live alone with the children under my own rules with maybe a partner who I saw regularly but didn't live with. Someone who I could share my life with but without all of the mess of finances and marriage and without the arguments over the toilet seat or who used the last of the milk.

This attitude has softened a little as time has gone on. I would now consider living with someone again and starting my life over with someone new, but it would have to be right. They would have to understand that I need rest and on occasion I won't leave my bed all weekend. They will need to understand about all my triggers, about all the medication I am on and what signs to look out for when I am about to trigger. Most importantly, they will need to let me be me. I would need them to accept the kids for who they are and accept that they are human and not in the slightest bit perfect. They would need to accept my parenting choices and realise I am doing my best. I would of course do the same in return.

On the flip side though, this would work in their favour. When I am resting and spending time by myself, they will be able to be themselves too. When I am resting, I need very little attention and they could therefore hide in their garage, go on long bike rides or spend the day playing computer games. It would be a win win situation!!

On the subject of re-marrying, I am not fussed either way. What I do know though if I was to ever marry again, I would want it to be a small intimate affair. Something personal and very close family and friends. I did the big wedding and I wouldn't want to do that again. There is no need. I would still want a pretty dress though, just not a big white one like I wore at my first wedding and it would have to have pockets!

# CHAPTER TWENTY - SLEEP AND MEDICATION

You might be wondering why these two subjects need a whole chapter. Well, sleep is a huge factor in staying stable and medication has saved my life.

Sleep is medication and I need medication to help me sleep. They both work hand in hand with each other.

I have a love hate relationship with sleep. I love sleep but I hate the fact I can't skip sleep by having a late night. I also have a similar relationship with medication. I hate taking it and its side effects but equally I couldn't function without it.

Both sleep and medication are huge factors in the recovery and treatment of bipolar and mental health conditons in general.

Sleep plays a vital role in good health and well-being throughout your life. Getting enough quality sleep at the right times can help protect your mental health, physical health, quality of life, and safety.

A hypermanic episode will usually mean no sleep for days at a time and we will need very little rest. During a depressive episode, sleep is all we do. I, for one will sleep for 18 hours a day, only waking to eat (junk food mainly) and collect the kids from school. The rest of the day I sleep, then all night I sleep.

Sleep, however, for those who suffer with bipolar is affected regardless of our mood.

We suffer from insomnia or hypersomnia. During a hypermanic episode there is a decreased need for sleep and my favourite is the REM stages of sleep which make dreams VERY vivid. I often sweat lots during the night no matter the temperature. A regular sleep routine is so important. Disrupted sleep can really aggravate bipolar.

**Too much sleep can trigger an episode. Not enough sleep can also trigger an episode. It's a balancing act.**

Then there is the medication. I am on several medications for my bipolar disorder that I take at certain times of the day. I am unable to sleep without a medication called Quetiapine. This is a mood stabiliser commonly used to treat bipolar, but it is also used as a sleep aid due to its sedating effect. If I forget to take it then this is recipe for disaster. I will literally lay awake for hours. It's not as simple as that though. If I take it too early, then the affects have usually worn off by the time its bedtime. Take it too late and ill struggle to wake up the next day and will usually be groggy all day.

Medication has been a life saver, quite literally. I am on three types of medication for my bipolar disorder. Lamotrigine twice a day, Fluoxetine twice a day and Quetiapine at night-time. I also have a few other medications for physical illnesses I have. I rattle and need one of those old people tablet boxes, so I remember to take them.

Without the medication and a good sleep routine I wouldn't be where I am today. I quite possibly wouldn't be here to tell the tale. I missed a few days of my medication once whilst on a weekend away with late nights and long days and it triggered an episode. **A sure sign I need medication and a proper sleep schedule.**

There are three different types of medication for bipolar – Anti-Depressants, Anti-Convulsant and Anti-Psychotics. I actually take one from each category.

The Quetiapine I take at night falls into the **antipsychotic** category. This prevents or at least reduces episodes of hypermanic episodes. This also sedates me and helps me ensure I can always get a good night's sleep. As we know, sleep is super important to me and other bipolar sufferers.

The **anti-depressant** I take is the Fluoxetine. This battles my depression and they ensure my mood is lifted. The only worry with this is it can often raise my mood too high – this is why I also have Quetiapine. Seems kind of pointless to have one to cancel out the other but I have tried to be off both and well, it didn't work.

The last bipolar medication I take is Lamotrigine. This is actually typically used for epilepsy and is an **anti-convulsant.** These also work as an anti-depressant, but it also prevents recurrent episodes. It is growing in popularity because of its effectiveness in mood maintenance.

One of the downsides, apart from all the side effects such as weight gain, I also have issues with many other medications being contraindicated. The Lamotrigine means I can't be on anything with progesterone (so that's 50% of long acting reversible contraception) and because I have suffered with migraines with aura in the past, I can't have anything with Oestrogen in them (so that's the other 50% of LARC's). To fall pregnant would have a huge impact on my mental health so I am currently waiting for a surgery date for Laparoscopic Sterilisation to remove my fertility all together.

Then there are the side effects which I need other medications to deal with. I suffer from IBS but this has got worse since all my other medications have been increased and so I am now on another medication to help with that. I rattle lots!

Now....about sleep.

I have always enjoyed sleeping. I would happily spend all day in bed at the weekends. This was possible when I was younger and before I had the children. I could rest when I wanted, have early nights and long lay ins.

Once they came along my sleep was heavily disrupted. I would have to nap when the children napped. I wouldn't be able to rest as and when I needed it. I had to take what I could and naturally my sleep cycles were all over the place and now when I look back, I realise so were my moods. The lack of sleep and becoming a new parent was definitely a trigger.

Bipolar sufferers will usually have their first episode in their late teens or early twenties. For some women though, giving birth and managing a new-born baby will trigger their first bipolar episode.

I was both.

I definitely had episodes as a teenager but as previously discussed I was then able to keep it at bay during my early adulthood and it lay dormant until I had the children and was most definitely triggered again by giving birth and having a baby.

# CHAPTER TWENTY-ONE - SUICIDE

**"You have the power to decide how your story ends"**

Such a tough subject to cover but definitely an important one. According to The Samaritans, deaths by suicide rose by 10.9% in the UK in 2018. There were 6507 suicides with three times more men committing suicide than females. This is because men are less likely to seek help.

People with bipolar disorder are at great risk for suicide if they are not getting treatment. The depressive phase of bipolar disorder is often very severe, and suicide is a major risk factor. In fact, people suffering from bipolar disorder are more likely to attempt suicide than those suffering from regular depression. Furthermore, their suicide attempts tend to be more lethal.

I personally have felt suicidal on numerous occasions and not just when I am low. I get suicidal during a mixed episode and I sometimes get low when I think about hard this disorder is and I very often wonder if it would be easier for everyone if I wasn't here.

When you visit a GP about your low mood, they will ask you if you have any suicidal thoughts. If the answer is yes, then they will delve further into these feelings.

There are two main types of suicidal thoughts. There is the persistent feeling of wanting to be dead but with no immediate plans to carry out a suicide. Then there are the suicidal thoughts that are accompanied by a plan of action. The latter is obviously the one that causes the biggest alarm.

I guess I have had both. If I am honest the thoughts are always there hiding in the background, but they increase during a low period. The thoughts will be intrusive, it will be all I can think about. I will wish I was dead, but I wouldn't actually consider doing anything to make that happen. On the other hand, I have made plans, researched ideas and I have made attempts. I have been at rock bottom several times and I am quite certain I will be there again more than once in the future.

There was the first attempt in 2001 when I was nineteen. Then there was the second attempt in 2019 after MR ended things. There was the time outside ER's house and I don't know how many times I have considered taking overdoses but didn't. I would regularly sit there with tablets in my hand after researching how many to take. The main reason I don't do it is the children of course but **usually it's because I am more scared about surviving than I am about dying.**

On top of this I binge drink and I often wish I would be in a car accident and have even considered causing one on a few occasions. I would never actually do this though as if I was in my car then I wouldn't be inebriated, and I would have some level of rational thought. It's the alcohol that makes my thoughts more irrational.

One occasion that no one knows about is a weekend I didn't have the children. I was bored, lonely, angry with ER and extremely fed up with life, so, I got in my car with the full intention of driving my car off a bridge. I ended up driving for 6 hours doing over 200 miles and eventually drove home when it became clear I didn't have the guts to actually do it. I had cried all the tears I had and arrived home exhausted but at least I was alive.

Many say suicide is the coward's way out. They clearly haven't been staring at a paracetamol packet in so much pain that it's the only way they can consider ending the agony.

**"People who die by suicide don't want to end their life; they want to end their pain"**

# CHAPTER TWENTY-TWO – THE STIGMA

**"Having a mental health disorder isn't easy and it's even harder when people assume you can just get over it"**

Unfortunately, not everyone understands mental health problems.

Stigma is.....a mark of disgrace associated with a particular circumstance, quality, or person. There is stigma over many things such as race, wealth and poverty, sexual orientation and unfortunately mental health.

This stigma means many people do not get the help they need until it is too late. They are too ashamed to seek help and support.

The most commonly held beliefs are that people with mental health conditions are dangerous, have drug dependence and/or they are self-inflicted. Those who have no understanding of the matter believe that those with mental health conditions are simply seeking attention.

It is often assumed that there can't be anything wrong because their life is perfect. There is the misconception that only those who are suffering physical illnesses, those who are poor or those who have suffered a loss have a reason to be depressed.

That's the thing about depression and other mental health conditions. Some people think depression is trivial and not a genuine health condition. They're wrong. It is a real illness with real symptoms. Depression is not a sign of weakness or something you can snap out of by pulling yourself together. When you are depressed, you feel persistently sad for weeks or months, rather than just a few days.

Of course, no one is saying that you can't be depressed because you are ill or have suffered a loss, but this is known as reactive or situational depression.

Situational depression is a short-term, stress-related type of depression. It can develop after you experience a traumatic event or series of events. Situational depression is a type of adjustment disorder. It can make it hard for you to adjust to your everyday life following a traumatic event. It's also known as reactive depression.

Clinical depression manifests itself regardless of one's home life and how great that is. Even Prince Harry has suffered from depression and many A-List celebrities have also suffered and many have taken their lives. Many wouldn't understand that, considering they all have lots of money and a life that many consider perfect.

Depression doesn't discriminate. One's money, success, skin colour, gender or social standing is irrelevant in the face of mental illness. Privilege and depression are not mutually exclusive and sometimes the ones shining the brightest are often in the most pain. People like Vincent Van-Gogh, Winston Churchill and Abraham Lincoln are all said to have suffered bipolar. Many other creative and intelligent celebrities such as musicians, artists, actresses, scientists and authors, suffer with the disorder. Does this I am super clever and creative??!

I mentioned that MC was originally unsupportive of my depression and he was on the "snap out of it" team and was one of those who believed by admitting you were suffering from depression meant you are weak. He came around when I was diagnosed, and he saw how well I was now doing on the various medications I take. He is now super supportive.

Another family member, however, wasn't as supportive. She refused to believe my diagnosis. The 4 different psychiatrists and 3 different GP's I had seen throughout the process were apparently wrong, and I just needed to get myself out of bed and 'grow up'. There wasn't anything wrong with me. I was simply seeking attention.

She didn't stop here though. She told my mother that I was not allowed an opinion on the way my Gran was cared for because my mental health condition meant I wasn't reliable or stable enough to be worth listening to. This is the same auntie who refused to admit to many that she had a disabled brother.

To say I was upset was an understatement. This is also the same auntie who I was extremely close to growing up. The same auntie who would regularly comfort me when I was down or had had an issue at home.

She had an issue with being associated or related to anyone with mental health conditions. I don't care what she thinks anymore, 7 health care professionals and the changes in me from taking medication can't be wrong but at the time I was very upset.

Thankfully everyone else in my life has been nothing but supportive. I do understand how hard it must be to empathise with someone who has depression if they have no prior experience of this or indeed have never had any of those feelings themselves but thankfully the stigma is now changing. With the help of websites such as bipolar.org.uk and mind.org.uk and campaigns such as Time to Change and Heads Together, more and more people are admitting their own mental health struggles and the stigma is slowly fading.

# CHAPTER TWENTY-THREE – NATURE VS NURTURE

We have discussed the fact that bipolar is hereditary and a lot of my 'quirks' as I like to call them definitely mirror that of my mother but equally many of them are as a result of the way I was raised and the childhood I had.

At university my dissertation was on Nature Vs Nurture.

*I opened the essay with the question...... "How much of who we are derives from our genes and human nature and how much is shaped by society and the environment. Does it all fall on nature, or is nurture responsible for all of who we are, or is it a combination of both?"*

Do people behave the way they do because of behaviours innate in them before they are born or have their ideas developed as a result of responses to the environment over time?

It can be proved with ease that physical features such as eye colour, height and even shoe size have developed from our genes, but the debate gets deeper and more complicated when it comes to our **behaviour, intelligence and personality.**

In my paper, I looked at three theorists: Jean Piaget, Maria Montessori and John Locke.

I discussed what they had considered important in the debate and what contributed to the human intellect, psychological make up and the thought process. What is innate and what develops through nurture?

Montessori (1964) believed that children are born with ideas and it is up to society to let them develop to their full potential with little or no influence and direction from adults. Children have, innate in them, the tools they require to develop and over time they will grow because of this inborn life within them and no amount of influence will change the pattern set out for them in their mother's womb. **She therefore believed nature was solely responsible.**

Locke (1689), believed environment, intervention and interaction play an essential and key factor in the development of a being and believed the mind was empty at birth. He believed that it is through experience, sensation and reflection that the mind comes to be furnished with ideas and language. **He was therefore on the 'nurture' side of the argument.**

Piaget (1929) was interested in the cognitive development of children and wanted to gain an insight into children's thoughts, language and understanding and believed that both social and biological factors combine at the beginning of the natural life. He believed it is neither simply nature nor simply nurture that aids development, but **both have their role to play in making us the individuals we are today.**

Is it personality, our ideas and notions OR the ability to take on new ideas **that is innate?**

Does a child inherit traits such as temperaments, self-esteem and interests or is this influenced through the society and culture?

So many things to consider when discussing the development of the human, can they possibly all be innate, or all gained from society?

In my dissertation, I chose to link these theories to how children were affected in education by both nature and nurture in the twenty first century but, how does all of this fit in with mental health diagnoses?

**What part does, nature and nurture have to play, in our mental health?**

I believe they both have a part to play. I have trust issues as does my mother, but do I have these because they are a learnt behaviour, a result of my troubled childhood or was I born with an untrusting personality? In my case, probably all three had a part to play.

My mother had her own troubled childhood where she would have reacted through 'nurture' and she would have carried this into her own adulthood, and I would have learnt these coping behaviours from my mother when I was a child. **Nurture.**

On the flip side, we both must have some element of an unstable personality in our nature. I know people who have dealt with much more in their lives and yet, do not react in a suicidal and untrusting way to these stressful situations like my mother and I do. **Nature**

We discussed how sleep is a huge trigger for me. If I don't get rest and a decent night's sleep, then I trigger. My brain is wired in a way that means lack of sleep will result in a hypermanic episode. So, this is a combination of both nature and nurture. I then have to use the tools I have learnt to control my nature. **Nature (my brain) and Nurture (the lack of sleep).**

I believe, therefore, particularly in the case of mental health that both play a part.

Ridley (2004) considered the idea that genes are not just from the infant's immediate family (parents) but from many years and generations before them. A child who comes into the world today inherits a set of genes and learns many lessons from experience, but she acquires something else too; the words, the thoughts and the tools that were invented by other people far away or long ago. **Past, present and indeed future create us and make us who we are**. What an infant brings with him or her is irreversible. This comes from their parents and ancestors before that, whereas society is the provider of nurture

So, in conclusion it is highly likely that both genetics and society play an equal role in the overall creation of the 'individual' and what makes us who we are. Personality, traits, tolerance and even some interests are inherited (genetic) and even the way we interact with the environment could be inherited.

The way our genes unravel is due to the environment and society. Trends, policies and peer pressure are all down to the era one is living in. Whilst you may have the same 'personality' as members of your family; the rest is down the societal influences of the time.

# CHAPTER TWENTY-FOUR – ALL ABOUT ME

So, you know about my crazy ways, my illness and how I manage that but what makes me, me? I am more than just my illness. I am more than just medication.

***"I am more than my scars"***

I spend so much of my time nowadays trying to not trigger, that my illness becomes the whole of me. I am unable to escape it and forget. My illness however is a small part of me.

I love sewing and eating chocolate. I love to go camping as much as possible and I love to get out in the forest. I love that I have two healthy children and I love being a cat mummy too. I love creating and there is nothing more relaxing than sitting there surrounded by fabric and coming up with something pretty to make. I just love crafts in general and I love making and designing things.

I love going to the zoo. I love giraffes and I love scones with clotted cream (jam first with cream on top!). Most things I wear are floral and I love wearing dresses. My favourite colour is purple, and I love butterflies. I would wear flip flops all year round if I could (I did when I was in Malaysia!) and I love travelling. I love reading memoirs and medical themed novels.

I have a collection of badges that I still add to and I love bunting. Lots of lots of bunting. I like pretty things and yet, I love practical things too. I don't wear makeup unless it's a special occasion and if I wear nail varnish, I will pick it off. I don't wear jewellery except a bracelet sometimes. I love making jewellery though. I have an obsession with bags. I have many, many bags and I am always adding to the collection even if I don't need to.

I love learning new medical terminology and learning in general. I love things that match and I love things to be tidy. I can't have things that are odd, and I, hate odd numbers. I love a road trip and fun weekends away. I love my bed and I love watching Grey's Anatomy on repeat.

I love cuddles and being stroked. I love being hugged just because and I love snuggling up with a movie. I love lazy days and I love productive days. I love everything to have a home and my desk has to be neat and tidy at work. I love food I shouldn't, and I love a good cup of tea. I love biscuits and cake a little too much, but I do love a nice banana as well and a roast dinner with lots of vegetables.

I love lists, more lists and even more lists. I love

spreadsheets and writing. I love to play Scrabble and I love to clean the house. I love making cakes and I love wine. I love chicken korma and a decent mint sauce with onion bhajis, I love wearing my pyjamas and I love my hot tub. I love my garden and living in a village.

I love waffles with toffee sauce and banana ice-cream, and I love pancakes. I love Celine Dion and Whitney Houston. I love my tattoos and want more and I love sleeping.

**But most importantly, I love people who make an effort and I love those who care for me when I don't even care for myself.**

# CHAPTER TWENTY-FIVE – EUPD, BIPOLAR OR MY PERSONALITY?

I briefly mentioned, in Chapter 17, how my bipolar disorder, the traits of EUPD and my actual personality will all cross over and, because of this it can be hard to distinguish whether the way I am feeling is because of my disorders or due to my personality traits.

The problem with mood disorders is, that, they take away our ability to see ourselves. We question whether the feelings we are feeling are really us or the illness.

The reason for this chapter is because, quite recently, I found myself in a situation where whilst I reacted in a way most people would, this reaction was called into question because of my mental health conditions.

I was feeling quite rightly very sad and confused about a negative situation that was happening in my life and when I tried to explain this to the relevant person I was asked **'are you feeling this way and are you misinterpreting what has been said**

**because of your mental health condition'**. This was quite insulting. The issue, I felt, was therefore simply dismissed because I couldn't possibly feel like this and it must simply be, the mental health conditions making me feel this way.

I felt like this belittled my feelings and made me feel like I was overreacting. **I had to explain that no, on this occasion I am very much in control of my mood and this is ME talking, this is ME feeling this way.**

It got me thinking about other times when this has happened and, how in the past it has been assumed that I can't handle stress, that ill crack up or be unpredictable and unreliable. People often tip toe around me or assume I am weak.

I also get the feeling, that people think I am incapable of making logical and rational decisions but, **sometimes the decisions are made simply, because of my personality.** Remember my auntie saying this about my opinion on my Gran's care. I have a degree, a family, a good job and a home and as you know I had quite a strong relationship with my Gran but, my mental health conditions apparently made my opinion invalid.

And to top it off, it can be very irritating when someone asks you "have you been taking your medication lately?".

When people raise these questions it does, unfortunately get me thinking and doubting myself though.

When I suffer from low self-esteem, is this because of my EUPD or do I naturally have self-esteem issues. When I am in a good mood is this because I am hypermanic or is life just making me happy at that moment in time. When I enjoy a project and throw myself in to it, is this a symptom of hypermania or simply because I am excited about that project. When I am feeling sad am I on the brink of a depression or am I just feeling a little blue. Have I made those decisions because of the chemical imbalance in my brain?

I think it is important though, to remember that there is a difference between a symptom and my personality. **I am not the total sum of symptoms.** Despite the belief that people suffering from bipolar are always 'bipolar' and their mood is never stable this is not true. Bipolar sufferers can go months without any symptoms, and they will be their 'true self' during this time.

Bipolar disorder does not have to prevent a person from living a meaningful life, and it's certainly not a punchline or a way to explain someone's quick change of mind or mood or their feelings and opinions. Mood swings can happen for many different reasons including the weather, one's menstrual cycle and common medications. Even the 'moon' can cause a mood to switch even in the most stable of people. Moodiness can also occur with hormone disorders, autoimmune diseases and neurological problems.

When talking to a person with a mood disorder remember they are more than their diagnosis. It does not define who we are.

There is also a huge amount of irony in all of this. **When someone questions my ability, questions my opinion, questions an idea or decision...... this is all a TRIGGER.** I will go away and think about it. I will analyse and agonise about whether maybe, I AM making these decisions because I am on the brink of an episode.

Having bi-polar is quite exhausting.

# CHAPTER TWENTY-SIX – TODAY, THE YEAR 2020, THE FUTURE

*"Recovery is not one and done. It is a lifelong journey that takes place one day, one step at a time"*

The last few years have been a journey of self-discovery and the years ahead of me will still have their challenges but with the tools I've acquired, it should be easier to navigate.

I have learnt why I have always struggled with relationships, friendships and my self-esteem.

I discovered why my moods always swung between the extremes and why I react in a suicidal way when it comes to criticism.

*So, I have discussed what bipolar is, how it affects me and others and how I manage it* **but how does it make me feel?**

On the whole these days, I am coping well. I accept it is part of me and this is how life is going to be but, naturally there are times where I really wish it would go away and I could live a normal life.

I want to be able to sit down and rest in the evening without having to have the whole house clean and in order. I would like to not have an obsession with having to have things lined up. I would like to be able to leave the house without having to straighten the remote controls, make the beds, hoover the floor and tidy the sofas. I do this regardless of my mood (technically I do have a **mild** form of OCD) but it gets much, much worse when I am hypermanic.

I hate not being able to be overly spontaneous. I wish I could have late nights and long days without the possibility of triggering into an episode. This upsets me sometimes and I get frustrated. I wish I could be a normal mum and be consistent with my care. I wish I could take them places without methodical planning on taking my medication, ensuring I get adequate rest and don't return home too late so as to disrupt my evening routine.

I wish I didn't have to have such a rigid routine.

> **"I am fine, but I have bipolar. I am on several medications which constantly put me in touch with the illness I have. I'm never quite allowed to be free of that for a day"**

I often wonder, if I had been medicated from a younger age, whether my life would have gone in a very different direction and this bothers me sometimes. Would I have made some of the life choices I chose, or would I have ended up somewhere different? These questions are sometimes hard to think about but unfortunately these thoughts regularly enter my head, particularly when I am depressed.

Of course, on top of the bipolar disorder, I also have the traits of Emotional Unstable Personality Disorder (EUPD) and this isn't 'episode based', this is always there, lurking in the background. It affects my self-esteem, the way I see myself, the way I think people see me and how I react to change and rejection.

I struggle with having low self-esteem. I wish I could relax and not worry about what other people think of me but my anxiety is always there lurking in the background. I become very aware of people around me. Ironically my anxiety is worse when I am stable. My mind is 'straight' and so I think more.

I worry about making people unhappy so I will do anything I can to make someone else happy. Favourite ice-creams, the perfect meals, little gifts to show I listen to them, I would drive an hour for a quick kiss and cuddle. I am always thoughtful and caring. This is often to my detriment (AR for example) but its who I am. I struggle to think of myself. I struggle to let people down.

**"People with BPD can be exceptionally caring, compassionate, and affectionate"**

I also struggle to let people do too much for me. I'm low maintenance and I don't need big gestures. Of course, I am indeed human and of course female and so I do like the odd small gesture, little surprises, random compliments, dinner made for me, washing folded etc is all I need. All the little things that will go a long way to stabilising my anxiety and self-esteem and my knowledge that I am cared for.

> **"I despise my own hypersensitiveness which require so much reassurance. It is certainly abnormal to crave too much to be loved and understood"**

*Note – it is now 2020 and I am actually finally achieving some of this. I still have to clean and tidy when I have visitors and will stress if things aren't perfect when people come round but I can now leave the house leaving some mess if I have ran out of time. I am also starting to love myself for who I am. I am no longer obsessed with my weight and these days I am what I am. Whilst I obviously don't want to end up obese, I am happy with my curves and wobbly bits and know that my new attitude is healthier.*

My self-esteem is raising gradually, and I am able to leave the house without making my bed. I do have to hoover though (I have 6 cats who clearly have parties overnight and therefore who make quite a mess) and the remotes still have to be straight, but I am making huge progress. I am learning not to throw my whole heart and soul into everything I do. I am less likely to now leave myself open for rejection.

> *"Bad things happen, but you have to move past it. Leave it behind. The sooner, the better. Or it'll eat away at you and stop you from moving forward." Miranda Bailey, Grey's Anatomy*

### So, what does the future hold for me?

As with anyone, who knows. What I do know though, is I now have more control over it.

The future will have the usual ups and downs that life would bring regardless and I will keep on managing my disorder the best I can through sheer determination, with medication and a huge amount of self-awareness. I will still have bad times. I will still have days where I will have doubt over whether I can do 'life' anymore.

I now know though that it is up to me and only me to attempt to control my future and how it ultimately pans out. I am aware of my limitations and have the tools to cope when things do go slightly array. I will rest. I will make realistic plans.

I know some people have it harder than me and I realise I'm quite lucky in lots of respects. I know I have a roof over my head, a job, a family, healthy children and friends and so I haven't written this to make people feel sorry for me and provide me with sympathy. I originally wrote this as part of my therapy, as part of my recovery and as something I could refer back to on occasion. I find writing therapeutic and it helps with my memory.

I found I had lots to say though and so I have ended up writing it more formally to possibly one day be brave enough to share with others and show other bipolar sufferers and those with other mental health conditions that they aren't alone, and things do get better.

If you are reading this then I was clearly brave enough to share it with you.

## "The pages of yesterday cannot be revised but the pages of tomorrow are blank, and you hold the pen. Make it an inspiring story"

If there was one thing, I would say to someone who is struggling with their own mental health it would be 'please do not be ashamed to admit you are struggling"

The first step is to take yourself to see your GP. Mental Health is taken much more seriously these days and you will not be judged.

Tip – I used to write things down. If I couldn't talk at an appointment, I could at least show them that. Whether it be in a list, a note on your phone or a formal diary like I used to do, anything to help you speak out and get the help you might need.

Please do not suffer in silence. You are not weak. You are not attention seeking. The help is out there, you just have to be brave enough to accept it.

**Would I go back and do things differently?**

The answer is no.

I am who I am today because of my past and I believe this is who I was meant to be.

Whichever journey I took I would have ended up where I am today.

Life goes on.... life will tick along.

> *"The carousel never stops turning".*
> *Ellis Grey, Grey's Anatomy*

# CHAPTER TWENTY-SEVEN – CHANGES & CHALLENGES

Apologies if this chapter appears a little out of place but I originally finished this book in the summer of 2020 but, I didn't get it ready to publish until December 2020 when several changes had taken place. This was mainly in my employment status and I feel it's an important chapter to add to the end before publishing.

The year 2020 was a weird year for everyone but I managed to stay stable for most of the turbulence (also known as lockdown). Well, that was until I found myself getting a ¾ sleeve tattoo and resigning from my job!

Unfortunately, I triggered in October after a week off with suspected COVID and so the doctor signed me off work. It was during this time that I realised I was going round and round. I would be at work, they would trigger me, I would then be off and then I would head back to work and have to explain my time off. I would then be fine again, and the cycle would play out a few months later. I knew I needed to break this cycle and the only way to do this was to leave my role at the doctors.

I was absolutely terrified, but I had to do it.

I handed my notice in a few days after my sick note was extended another month and with no job to go to **but** with the confidence I would find **something.**

I applied for everything – cleaning, care, reception, even retail work – anything really. I just needed something to tide me over whilst I looked for my next real challenge. During the first week I applied for 16 jobs and I was lucky to be contacted for interview by 8 of them.

One of the roles I had applied for called me almost immediately and I had a phone interview the next day. Fast forward 2 weeks and I had attended a PMVA course, completed a couple of dozen online courses and had accepted a role as a mental health support worker/health care assistant at the nearby psychiatric hospital working with adolescents and young adults with eating disorders, depression, personality disorders and other mental health conditions. Some of these are informal patients and others are there under section 2 and 3 of the Mental Health Act.

Many have questioned whether this is right for me. The job involves shift work including nights which isn't overly good for my routine (or lack of it) and of course the subject itself has an opportunity to make me trigger but as I write this, I am sat watching a young girl with depression, anxiety and self-harm issues sleep and I just know I have made the right decision. Of course, time will tell but for the first time in a long time I feel like I am making a difference. I am hoping this will be the right decision and so far, I am very happy, and my old role is now a distant memory.

I have opted to do night shifts. This in theory isn't ideal but it appears to be working. I get to sleep in the day, no early starts and childcare is less of an issue which also resolves other issues such as school holidays, inset days and the children being poorly as I won't be working any school hours.

So, as we approach 2021, I am optimistic for an episode free year.......

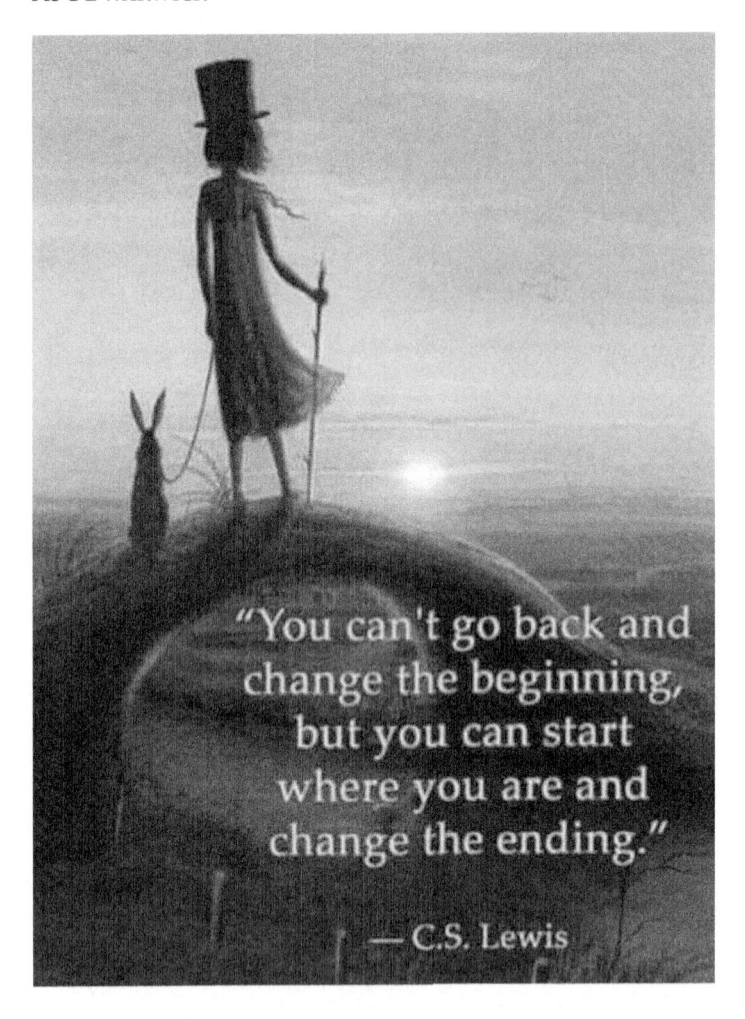

> "You can't go back and change the beginning, but you can start where you are and change the ending."
>
> — C.S. Lewis

# CHAPTER TWENTY-EIGHT – RELAPSE 2021

I have now been at my new place of work for just over 6 months and I am still loving it. I feel like I am doing something incredibly worthwhile and I look forward to every shift.

I enjoy seeing the young people and finding out about their day or days depending on when my last shift was. I have brought my love of crafts to the night shift and I love teaching them new tricks (sewing was a recent activity they enjoyed) and sharing my passions.

The reason for this chapter however, is because for the first time in many many months (9 months!) I have found myself **feeling suicidal**.

I really enjoy my job and life outside of work is pretty settled and I have lots to look forward to (my big 4-0 is fast approaching) but for some reason my brain is telling me to just give up on life.

**I have honestly considered an overdose on several occasions lately.**

As I type this I am thinking how it would just be

easier to just end my life. I am rubbish. I am stupid. No one likes me. I am lonely. I am scared. I want to die.

I know I wont go through with it but what if?

What if I just left the kids to live a better life with their dad?

What if I didnt have to spend my life worrying about triggering?

What if I am just not meant to be in this world?

I am just tired. So incredibly tired. I just don't want to be here anymore……..but I know this is just a blip and as always I will come out the other side.

It just sucks right now.

# REFERENCES

Locke, J, (1693), Essay Concerning Human Understanding

Montessori, M, (1964), The Montessori Method

Piaget, J, (1929), The Child's Conception of the World

Ridley, M, (2004), Nature Via Nurture: Genes, Experience and What makes us Human

www.mentalhealth.org.uk

www.bipolaruk.org

www.timetochange.co.uk

www.helpguide.co.uk

www.nhs.org.uk

www.mind.org.uk

www.psychcentral.com

www.headstogether.org.uk

Multiple quotes from Grey's Anatomy, ABC, First aired March 2005

Multiple quotes from Google searches, original

MS G L WARWICK

source and authors unknown